Black Earth

SELECTED POEMS AND PROSE

*

Osip Mandelstam

*

Translated from the Russian by Peter France

A New Directions Paperbook Original

Frontispiece: Osip Mandelstam (1891–1938), Russian State Archive of Literature and Art,
Moscow. Alamy Stock Photo.

Manufactured in the United States of America
First published as a New Directions Paperbook (NDP1505) in 2021

Library of Congress Cataloging-in-Publication Data
Names: Mandel'shtam, Osip, 1891–1938, author. | France, Peter, 1935– translator.
Title: Black earth : selected poems and prose / Osip Mandelstam ; translated
from the Russian by Peter France.
Description: New York, NY : New Directions Publishing, 2021.
Identifiers: LCCN 2020054980 | ISBN 9780811230971 (paperback) |
ISBN 9780811230988 (ebook)
Subjects: LCSH: Mandel'shtam, Osip, 1891–1938—Translations into English. |
LCGFT: Literature.
Classification: LCC PG3476.M355 B58 2021 | DDC 891.71/42—dc23
LC record available at https://lccn.loc.gov/2020054980

10 9 8 7 6 5 4 3 2 1

New Directions Books are published for James Laughlin
by New Directions Publishing Corporation
80 Eighth Avenue, New York 10011

ndbooks.com

CONTENTS

PROSE

Mandelstam has become an almost mythical figure of modern Russian poetry. In the English-speaking world this is due in part to the dramatic and tragic story of his life and death as told in the remarkable memoirs of his widow, Nadezhda Yakovlevna, translated by Max Hayward as *Hope Against Hope* (1970) and *Hope Abandoned* (1974). But above all there is the power and richness of his poetry, which for many readers make him the outstanding poet of twentieth-century Russia. He has been much translated, almost on a par with such stars as Horace and Baudelaire, and it was only after long hesitation that I added my offering in the form of a pamphlet, *Poems of Osip Mandelstam*, published by New Directions in 2015. The present volume is a revised and considerably enlarged edition of that pamphlet, to which I have added a little of Mandelstam's prose, memoirs of his Petersburg childhood, an essay written just after the Revolution, and extracts from three works of the early 1930s.

Osip Emilievich Mandelstam was born in Warsaw in 1891, the son of a leather merchant. The city of his childhood and youth was St. Petersburg, where his memoir *The Noise of the Times* shows him living in two very different worlds, what he calls the "Judaic chaos" of his family background and the imperial world of the Russian capital. Education gave him access to the heights of European culture; he studied at the prestigious Tenishev School (later attended by the young Vladimir Nabokov) and signed on in the Faculty of History and Philology at St. Petersburg University. Much of the period between 1907 and 1910 he spent as a student in western Europe (France, Germany, Italy), acquiring the classical culture which is at the heart of his writing.

He began his literary career under the tutelage of the Symbolist over-lord Vyacheslav Ivanov, and this early Symbolism left its mark on his first collection of poems, *Stone*, first published in 1913 and then in a much-enlarged second edition in 1916. Early poems in this volume echo the work of the nineteenth-century poet Fyodor Tyutchev, a favorite of the Sym-bolists, who was to remain an important influence. Tyutchev had seen the daylight world as a golden cover thrown over the essential abyss of night; he offers an exciting Romantic vision of the great flux of matter and time. In the majority of the poems in *Stone*, however, and indeed in the title chosen for the collection, we see Mandelstam writing against the chaos and emptiness evoked by Tyutchev. From about 1912, he was a member of the Acmeist group of poets, who advocated clarity, this-worldliness and the constructive principle. Although his own poetic path took him away from Acmeist positions, Mandelstam was to remain true to his Acmeist colleagues all his life, above all to Anna Akhmatova and to the memory of her husband Nikolay Gumilyov, who was shot in 1921 for alleged counter-revolutionary plotting.

His essay "The Morning of Acmeism," published in 1919, sets out these early positions. The Symbolists are dissatisfied with the world and with their own bodies, but the Acmeist poet is at home in his three-dimensional existence. Where they speak of the inadequacy of language, he welcomes the solidity of the word, which he will use as the raw material for his own constructions. Architectural images abound: building, writes Mandelstam, "means combating emptiness, hypnotizing space. The good arrow of a Gothic spire is aggressive because its whole purpose is to pierce the sky and reproach it for its emptiness." At the center of *Stone* are three poems devoted to great buildings, represented here by "Notre-Dame" and "The Admiralty," though these sit alongside light-hearted poems such as "Tennis" that evoke the elegant world of modern Petersburg society.

The treatment of Petersburg (or Petrograd, or Leningrad) is complex in Mandelstam's writing, as indeed in most Russian literature. Petersburg was his city, and at first he responded enthusiastically to the classical order imposed onto the chaos. After the October Revolution, in many of the poems in his second volume, *Tristia* (1922), he mourns the death of the old Petersburg, most openly perhaps in "We shall all meet again in Petersburg," and hauntingly in a series of poems where the theme of the lost word is interwoven with images of Psyche, Persephone, and the swallow returning to the world of shades. But already, in poems written before the Revolution, he had stressed the fragility of the city to which he gives the classical name "Petropolis." Later, in poems of the early 1930s such as "Leningrad," the city would become a place of fear.

Nor did he belong entirely to this classical, "imperial" world. The "Judaic chaos" from which he had emerged continued to inhabit him. In his "Fourth Prose," written in 1930 when he was harassed by writers whom he despised, he would write defiantly of his Jewish inheritance ("My blood, weighed down by the legacy of shepherds, patriarchs, and kings . . ."). In his writing, however, the Jewish tradition is not opposed to the classical, but reconciled with it in defense of human values. Both are connected with the South, the Mediterranean, which was the focus of what he called the "nostalgia for world culture." Like many writers of northern Europe, he was haunted by the image of a sunlit world of human dimensions. "Hellenism," he once wrote, "is the conscious surrounding of man by utensils rather than indifferent objects, indeed the transformation of these objects, humanizing the surrounding world and warming it with the subtlest teleological warmth." This Hellenism is connected with ancient Greece of course, and with Ovid's Rome and Dante's Tuscany, but also with places that Mandelstam actually knew, notably the Crimea, the scene for several of his poems, including the magnificent "The thread of golden honey flowed from the jar."

In 1922, Mandelstam married Nadezhda Yakovlevna Khazina, who subsequently accompanied him into internal exile and devoted herself to preserving his work after his death. By 1922 he was realizing with increasing clarity that the new order was inimical to his existence. In some ways he seems at first to have welcomed the Revolution, even if ambiguously (See "Let's honor freedom's twilight, brothers"). As a worker in words, he would have liked to belong with the Russian people, those who carried the real Russian language, and in his 1921 essay "The Word and Culture," he defiantly claimed a central role for poetry in the new Revolutionary society, but in a way that few of the new cultural bosses could accept or even understand. A few years later, he replied mildly but prophetically to a questionnaire, "I feel myself indebted to the Revolution, but I bring it gifts that it does not yet need." He was increasingly criticized and excluded from the official literary world. Like other lyric poets—such as Pasternak—he virtually stopped writing poetry between 1925 and 1930, though he remained active as a translator. In 1928, however, he was able to publish a small group of poems from 1923–24 that give memorable expression to the perception of a broken, or divided, culture, notably the magnificent and difficult longer poems "The Age," "One Who Finds a Horseshoe," "Slate Pencil Ode," and "January 1, 1924."

According to Nadezhda Mandelstam, it was only in 1930, when he broke with official Soviet culture in his violently satirical "Fourth Prose," that he was able to start writing poetry again. From this period on, very few of his writings were published (one notable exception being *Journey to Armenia*). His livelihood was precarious; he and his wife were forced into a sort of nomadic existence, mainly in Leningrad and Moscow, depending a good deal on the kindness of friends. The poems he composed were preserved either orally, memorized by his wife and by friends, or in manuscript or typescript. There are poems of many kinds in the Leningrad and Moscow "notebooks" that contain the work written from 1930 to 1934: some light and jaunty, some bafflingly hermetic, some grimly impressive, and some as rich and as beautifully constructed as the poems of *Tristia*. Many of them read like personal (and therefore sometimes obscure) responses to a changing environment, but through all of this persists the ideal of a sunlit Mediterranean world. The poem addressed to Ariosto is an example of this; in the 1930s Mandelstam (following his Russian predecessor Batyushkov, the subject of another memorable lyric homage) was drawn deeply into the work of the poets of the Italian Renaissance. He translated some Petrarch, and in his "Conversation about Dante" produced a remarkable defense and definition of the poetic word.

Although by this time there could be no question of any official literary position for him, he felt the obligation—in accordance with established Russian tradition—to confront the realities of his life and society through his poetry. Often this was done obliquely; in the Ariosto poem he praises the diplomatic foxiness of the Italian master, and he himself often seems to be seeking refuge in obscurity. At times, however, he speaks plainly and defiantly, notably so in the infamous "Stalin epigram." Returning from a visit to the South in 1933, during which he had been appalled by the poverty and hardship resulting from collectivization, he wrote a fierce and funny little poem about the sadistic dictator and his court ("We live without touching the homeland beneath us"). The poem was recited in apparently friendly circles, but someone must have informed, and Mandelstam was arrested, imprisoned, and interrogated. He was "lucky" and got away with three years' internal exile in the provinces. First he was sent to the remote town of Cherdyn in the Urals; here, driven half mad by what he had undergone, he threw himself out of a hospital window. Then he was moved to the city of Voronezh in the black-earth region of Russia some 350 miles southeast of Moscow.

In Voronezh, far from home and living as usual in great poverty, he wrote his last and some of his best poetry, grouped in three "notebooks." His vision of the world remains in many ways the same, but what Joseph Brodsky calls "the character of the verse" is transformed, particularly when compared with the poems of *Tristia*. Brodsky writes in his essay "The Child of Civilization": "Its sublime, meditative, caesuraed flow changed into a swift, abrupt, pattering movement. His became a poetry of high velocity and exposed nerves, sometimes cryptic, with numerous leaps over the self-evident with somewhat abbreviated syntax. And yet in this way it became more a song than ever before, not a bardlike but a birdlike song, with its sharp unpredictable turns and pitches, something like a goldfinch tremolo."

Most of the poems of what is called the first Voronezh notebook, written in the spring and summer of 1935, show Mandelstam trying to come to terms with his recent experiences and his new environment. They are very varied, expressing for instance the rapid fluctuations of his reactions to exile, amazed admiration of the black earth, nostalgia for Moscow, wry joking at his situation, nightmarish memories of the long river journey to and from Cherdyn, attempts to come to terms with Soviet reality, forebodings of disaster, and perhaps, above all, a continuing faith in poetry and the poetic word. The second and third notebooks contain poems written between December 1936 and May 1937, often enigmatic, but jagged, image-studded, and grippingly sonorous—a peak in his writing. Again, they touch on many different themes and express many different moods, but almost all show the same realistic engagement with the actual world that had been growing in Mandelstam since the early 1920s. The world is seen as a place of living beauty (memorably represented by the goldfinch), but also as a place of hardship and fear. Mandelstam was an ill man at this time and felt he had not long to live. He was constantly aware of the threat emanating from the Kremlin, and many of the poems are sparks struck off in protest as Mandelstam tried to write an ode to the dictator.

One memorable short poem, "What can we do with the deadness of the plains," ends with a vision, reminiscent perhaps of Yeats's "Second Coming," of "the Judas of the peoples still to come." Mandelstam is writing not only of the threat to himself, but to peoples of the future. It was another year before he fell victim to the beast. After returning from exile, he and his wife were driven from place to place. In May 1938 he was arrested for the second time and despatched to the labor camps. From near Vladivostok he wrote to his brother and wife in October 1938: "I'm in very poor health, utterly exhausted, emaciated, almost unrecognizable, but I don't know if there's any point in sending things, food and money; give it a try though, I'm freezing for lack of clothes. My darling Nadenka, are you alive, sweetheart? You, Shura, write to me straight away about Nadya. This is a transit camp. They didn't send me to Kolyma. I may spend the winter here." But he did not last the winter; he died at the end of December 1938 and was buried in a mass grave.

For many years to come Mandelstam was officially a non-person in Russia, but not forgotten. Much of his unpublished poetry survived orally, having been committed to memory by his wife and friends, and from the 1950s onwards he began to be published again, notably in the *Collected Works* (*Sobranie sochinenii*, 1955) edited and published in New York by

G. P. Struve and B. A. Filippov, the first edition in Russian of their great four-volume collection published between 1967 and 1981. My translations are for the most part based on this edition, but it should be noted that the text of many of Mandelstam's poems, especially the later ones, is far from stable, with the reader being offered one or more variants. In particular, for two important poems, "The Age" and "Slate Pencil Ode," I have followed the version given in the American edition rather than that found in the latest Russian edition, which adds another stanza to the former and removes a stanza from the latter.

There are numerous translations of Mandelstam in English. One of the earliest and most important of these, the *Selected Poems* published in 1973 by Clarence Brown and W. S. Merwin, was famously attacked by Brodsky, for whom it was a betrayal to replace the original Russian meters with free verse. This position was vigorously rebutted by the French poet Yves Bonnefoy, but the debate goes on; these are the eternal questions about the translation of poetry, to which all translators have to work out their own answers. My translations are generally "close," seeking to suggest as much as possible, not only of meanings, but also of the shape, rhythms, and verbal density of the often enigmatic originals. With a few exceptions, Mandelstam's poems are richly rhymed; without emulating him in this, I have used a variety of full rhymes, slant rhymes, internal rhymes, assonance, and alliteration in attempting to recreate in English a poetry that appeals equally to the inner eye and ear.

In working on Mandelstam I have been aided and encouraged by many people—too many to name here. Numerous scholars have helped me to understand more fully these often difficult poems; let me just mention the pioneering work of Clarence Brown, the illuminating insights offered by Kiril Taranovsky, Omry Ronen, Gregory Freidin, Boris Gasparov, Jennifer Baines and others, and the recent summa by Andrew Kahn, *Mandelstam's Worlds* (Oxford, 2020). I have profited greatly by the example of earlier translators, among whom I hope it is not invidious to give a special mention to James Greene and for the prose, Clarence Brown. And above all, a big thank you to all the friends who have read these translations and given me criticism, suggestions, and encouragement, in particular Boris

Dralyuk, Robert Chandler, Andrew Kahn, Angela Livingstone, Siân Reynolds, and Antony Wood, together with Jeffrey Yang and his colleagues at New Directions. And finally, a deep bow to the stupendous figure of Osip Mandelstam.

—PETER FRANCE
EDINBURGH, SCOTLAND

POEMS

*

The cautious muffled sound
of a fruit torn from a tree
amid the midnight song
of deep woodland peace . . .

1908

*

No need to speak of anything,
no call to teach a single thing,
and the dark animal soul
feels sad or good as seasons roll:

It does not wish to teach a thing,
it cannot speak of anything,
and, like a young dolphin, it will play
in the grey gulfs of everyday.

1909

SILENTIUM

She has not yet been born, and still
she is both music and the word,
and therefore the inviolable
union of all that lives on earth.

The ocean's breasts breathe peacefully,
but like a mad thing, day is bright,
and the foam's pale lilac lies
within a clouded bowl of light.

So let my lips now make their own
the dumbness of the dawn of time
like a note that is crystalline
in its original purity!

Aphrodite, still be foam,
let words be music once again,
and heart for heart still suffer shame,
with pristine life again made one!

1910

*

Keen hearing stretches out a sail,
emptiness fills the widening eyes,
and through the quietness swims by
the noiseless choir of midnight birds.

I am as poor as nature is,
I am as simple as the sky,
my freedom is as tenuous
as voices of the midnight birds.

I see the moon devoid of life,
the sky more deathly than a sheet;
your eerie and distempered world
is welcome to me, emptiness!

1910

Out of the evil, sticky deep
I grew and rustled like a reed,
inhaling a forbidden life
with passion and a languid greed.

And unobserved by all, I sink
into a cold and clammy home,
and here the short-lived autumn hours
whisper their welcome as I come.

Cruel injury makes me glad
and in a dreamlike life, alone,
I secretly envy the whole world,
and secretly love everyone.

1910

*

Stretching tight the silken threads
on the iridescent shuttle,
now begin your lesson, supple
fingers, begin your magic spells!

Ebbing and flowing of the hands,
movements of monotony,
you exorcize without a doubt
a panic terror of the sun,

when the broad palm, blazing like
a seashell, for a time grows dim
as the pull of shadows draws it in,
then moves back into rosy fire!

1911

*

No, not the moon, a brightly lit clock face
shines down on me, and how am I to blame
for seeing the milky weakness of the stars?

And I can't stomach Batyushkov's conceit:
"What time is it?" they asked him here on earth,
and his reply was just: "Eternity."

1912

I hate the steady gleam
of the monotonous stars.
Welcome, my ancient dream—
arrow thrust of the tower!

Stone, spread yourself in lace,
become a spider's web:
with a fine needle pierce
the heavens' empty breast.

My turn too will come—
I sense the wings stretched taut,
but where then can I aim
the arrow of living thought?

Perhaps I'll take my path
and time, then come back here:
There—I could not love,
here—love is my fear.

1912

NOTRE-DAME

Here, where a Roman judge once judged an alien people,
stands a basilica, fresh minted, full of joy;
as Adam long ago stood tall and flexed his sinews,
its muscles ripple through the light crisscrossing vaults.

Outside its walls you feel the hidden calculation—
like a saddle girth the power of arches planned
to hold in check the ponderous mass of stone from crushing
the walls, and neutralize the vaults' wild battering ram.

A primal labyrinth, unfathomable forest,
the reasoned vertigo that fills the gothic soul,
the power of Egypt, the humility of Christians,
an oak next to a reed—under the plumb-line's rule.

But, fortress Notre-Dame, as more attentively
I gazed and studied your prodigious frame,
I thought more and more: let the mass be stubborn,
I too shall shape it to magnificence one day.

1912

PETERSBURG STANZAS

to N. Gumilyov

Over the yellowness of government buildings
an endless murky blizzard swirled away,
and once again the lawyer with a flourish
flings on his coat and climbs into his sleigh.

The steamers are laid up for winter. Under
bright sun the thick glass of the cabin burns,
and, like a battleship in dock, the monster
that we call Russia rests its heavy bones.

On the Neva are flags of countless nations,
the admiralty, sun, and quietness;
and the stiff porphyry of state occasions
like a coarse scratchy haircoat breathes distress.

The northern snob must bear a heavy burden—
the ennui that Onegin felt of old;
on Senate Square the snowdrifts like a bulwark,
the smoke of bonfires and the bayonet's cold . . .

The yawls have drawn up water, and the seagulls
have filched the hemp heaped up along the dock,
where, vending their sweet potions and their breadrolls,
only the operatic peasants walk.

Into the mist fly the long lines of motors;
the quiet, proud pedestrian walking late—
poor Eugene—is ashamed he has no money,
inhales the petrol fumes and curses fate.

1913

THE ADMIRALTY

In the northern capital a dusty poplar languishes,
a transparent dial is tangled in the leaves,
and in the dark greenery, frigate, acropolis,
it shines from afar, a brother to sky and sea.

An airy vessel, mast of touchiness,
a rule for those who follow where Peter trod,
it teaches: beauty's no whim of a demigod,
but the keen reckoning of a joiner's eye.

Mastery of four elements gladdens the heart,
but human freedom has set up a fifth.
Is not the dominance of space denied
by the chaste lines of this created ark?

Capricious jellyfish cling angrily,
like plows abandoned anchors lie and rust—
and lo, the bonds of three dimensions break
and universal seas are opened up.

1913

TENNIS

In among the garish dachas
where a squeezebox staggers by,
balls are flying between matches,
magic bait to tempt the eye.

Who, subduing his rude fury,
in Alpine snow from head to foot,
dares to meet a pert valkyrie
in Olympic tournament?

Strings of the lyre are too decrepit:
the Englishman forever young
built and gave the world a racket
strung with golden strings and strong!

Lightly armed, he joins the battle
in a ritual of play;
as if in ancient days an Attic
warrior loved his enemy!

May. The thunderclouds in tatters.
Lifeless greenery hugs the soil.
Everywhere the horns of motors—
Lilac scent and engine oil.

From a jug the cheery sportsman
gulps spring water, clear and fresh,
and again the war goes forward,
with a glimpse of naked flesh!

1913

AKHMATOVA

Half-turned-away and sorrowful,
she gazed at others' unconcern;
the pseudo-classicizing shawl
slipped from her shoulders, turned to stone.

An ominous voice—a bitter draft—
soul giving vent to inner rage:
so—Phaedra in her burning wrath—
Rachel once stood upon the stage.

1914

*

Orioles in the woods—the only measure
the length of vowels in the tonic verses.
But one day only in the year does nature
brim with duration like Homeric meter.

The day yawns wide as if in a caesura
with peace and long-drawn work from dawn to night;
in the fields bullocks, and a golden leisure
to draw from reeds the wealth of a full note.

1914

I have not heard the tales of Ossian
nor have I tasted the old wine.
Why then this misty glimpse of heather
spread beneath Scotland's bloodstained moon?

I seem to hear in the grim silence
the clashing calls of harp and crow,
and all the while the windblown tartans
of clansmen gleam beneath the moon.

I have been given a blessed heirloom—
the wandering songs of foreign bards;
now knowingly we have the freedom
to scorn the dullness of our days.

And maybe through the generations
these many treasures will come down,
and scalds will make those foreign ballads
and will recite them as their own.

1914

*

Sleeplessness. Homer. Sails stretched tight.
I've read half through the catalogue of ships—
that long processional of cranes in flight
which once rose skyward over Greece.

An arrowhead of cranes aimed at a foreign land—
a godlike foam adorns the heads of kings—
where are you flying? If there was no Helen,
what would Troy be to you, Achaean men?

The sea and Homer, all things move in love.
Which should I listen to? Homer now is silent,
and like an orator the black sea roars
and with a crash breaks on my pillow.

1915

*

I shall not see the celebrated *Phèdre*
in the old-fashioned many-storied theater
with its high smoke-blackened gallery
by the guttering candles' light.
And, indifferent to the actors' bustle
as they gather in their harvest of applause,
I shall not hear across the footlights,
winged with its double rhyme the line:

—How these vain veils have grown repugnant to me . . .

The theater of Racine! A mighty barrier
divides us from this other universe;
between that world and ours there lies a curtain
that troubles us with its deep folds.
Classical shawls fall from the shoulders,
molten with suffering the voice grows stronger,
and the word white-hot with indignation
is tempered by the flame of grief . . .

I am too late for Racine's high festival!

Again the decaying posters rustle,
faint smells of orange peel drift out,
and as from the lethargy of ages
my neighbor stirs and says to me:
—Exhausted by Melpomene, her madness,
in this life it is peace alone I long for;
let us go before the jackal audience
tears the Muses limb from limb!

Oh if some Greek could see our pastimes . . .

1915

19

*

—How the splendor of these veils and this adornment
weighs on me in the midst of my dishonor!

    —Rocky Troezen will see
    a famous calamity,
    the royal palace steps
    will blush red with shame,
    . . . .
    . . . .
    and for the lovesick mother
    a black sun will rise.

—If only it was hate that boiled within my breast—
but see how the confession escaped me unawares.

    —With a black flame Phaedra burns
    in the brightness of day.
    A funeral torch smokes
    in the brightness of day.
    Fear your mother, Hippolytus:
    Phaedra—night—lies in wait for you
    in the brightness of day.

—With my black love I have defiled the sun . . .
. . . .

    —We are afraid, we do not dare
    help the king in his grief.
    Wounded by Theseus,

night has fallen on him.
But we with a funeral dirge,
bringing home the dead,
will sing to rest the black sun
of wild unsleeping passion.

1916

*

Cold chills my body. The transparent spring
decks out Petropolis in pale green down,
but Neva's water, like a jellyfish,
inspires a faint revulsion in my soul.
On the embankment of the northern river
dragonflies and metallic beetles hover,
the fireflies of motor cars flash by
and the gold pins of stars gleam in the sky,
but there is no star able to destroy
the heavy emerald of the moving sea.

1916

*

We'll die in crystalline Petropolis,
where we are governed by great Proserpina.
With every breath the fatal air we sip,
and every hour is death's fatal arena.

Goddess of ocean, menacing Athena,
take off your powerful stone helmet. Yes,
we'll die in crystalline Petropolis,
where it's not you who rules, but Proserpina.

1916

In a deep sleigh, with straw spread for a litter,
the fateful matting barely kept us dry
from Sparrow Hills to that familiar chapel
the day we rode through Moscow's immensity.

But kids are playing knuckle-bones in Uglich,
it smells of bread left cooling in the oven.
They drive me through the streets, my head uncovered,
and in the little church three candles burn.

Not three candles were burning, but three meetings,
and one of them was blessed by God alone,
there will not be a fourth, Rome is far distant,
and he has never felt a love for Rome.

The sleigh went bumping over the black potholes,
the crowds were coming home from a day out,
the skinny peasant men, the bitter women
stood at the gates, shifting from foot to foot.

Black flocks of birds darken the dripping distance,
the hands are manacled, swollen and raw;
the young prince is driven in, numb and unfeeling,
and they have set alight the saffron straw.

1916

Doubting the wonder of the resurrection
we wandered through the cemetery.
—You know, the earth in all directions
brings back those distant hills to me
. . . .
. . . .
where Russian land reaches its last limits
over a black and thundering sea.

From the monastery hill-slopes
a wide-flung meadow stretches out.
I did not want to leave Vladimir
and its expanses for the south,
but to remain in this dark quarter
of wooden, superstitious faith,
to be with this dark nun forever—
that would have been a living death.

I kiss the elbow, deeply sunburnt,
the forehead with its waxy air.
I know: it has remained white under
a shadowy lock of golden hair.
I kiss the wrist where from a bracelet
a slender strip of skin is pale.
The scorching summers of Crimea
are enough to work this miracle.

How very quickly you grew swarthy,
and then came forth to our poor Saviour
and kept on kissing, never tiring,
though you were proud in Moscow days.
And now only the name is left us—

for years to come a wondrous sound.
So take from me what I have sprinkled
from palm to palm—these grains of sand.

1916

*

The thread of golden honey flowed from the jar
so weighty and slow that our hostess had time to declare:
Here in melancholy Tauris, where fate has brought us,
we are not bored at all—and glanced back over her shoulder.

On all side the rites of Bacchus, as if the world
held only watchmen and dogs, not a soul to be seen—
the days roll peacefully by like heavy barrels:
Away in the hut are voices, you can't hear or reply.

We drank tea, then went out to the huge brown garden,
dark blinds were down like lashes over the eyes,
we walked past the white columns to look at the vineyard
where the somnolent hills are coated in airy glass.

I said: The vines are alive like ancient battles,
where curly horsemen are fighting in tangled order,
in stony Tauris the science of Hellas lives on—
and the noble rusty array of golden acres.

And in the white room quiet stands like a spinning wheel,
smells of vinegar, paint and wine that is fresh from the cellar.
Remember, in that Greek house, the much loved wife—
Not Helen—the other wife—how long she embroidered?

Golden fleece, oh where are you now, golden fleece?
All the journey long the heavy sea waves were loud,
and leaving his ship, his sails worn out by the seas,
full of space and time, Odysseus came home.

1917

27

Let's honor freedom's twilight, brothers,
honor the mighty twilight year.
Beneath the seething nighttime waters
the leaden weight of nets is sunk.
Into the dull years of stagnation
you rise up—people, judge, and sun.

Let's honor, too, the fateful burden
the people's leader, all in tears, accepts.
Honor the darkening load of power
in its unbearable dead weight.
Who has a heart, must hear your vessel,
time, as it sinks to the seabed.

We have bound fast the warlike legions
of swallows—and at once the sun
is no more to be seen, and nature,
living and moving, chirps its song.
Through nets—the obscure face of twilight—
no sun is seen, the earth sails on.

What of it, then, let us attempt it,
the great unwieldy turn of the wheel.
The earth sails on. Men, show your courage.
Plowing a furrow through the seas,
we shall remember in cold Lethe
we paid ten heavens for this earth.

May 1918

TRISTIA

I have studied the science of farewells
in the bareheaded grief of night.
The oxen chewing and the long-drawn wait,
the last hour of the city watch.
I know the ritual of the cockcrow night
when, lifting their load of travelers' grief,
the tear-filled eyes peered beyond sight
and muses' song mingled with women's tears.

Who can tell, when the word "farewell" is spoken,
what kind of separation lies before us,
what is foretold by the cock's exclamation,
when a fire is lit on the acropolis,
and at the dawn of some new life,
while the ox chews lazily in the stall,
why the cock, the herald of new life,
flaps his wings high on the city wall.

I love the rituals of weaving:
the shuttle scurrying, the spindle's hum,
and look, like swan's down, running barefoot
Delia is flying out to greet us!
Oh, what a threadbare life we lead,
how pitifully poor the words of joy!
All has been seen, all will be seen again,
only the moment of recognition is sweet.

So be it: a transparent figurine
is lying on a clean earthenware dish
like the skin of a squirrel stretched out flat,
a girl bends over the wax and stares.
It's not for us to guess Greek Erebus,

wax is for women what bronze is for men:
only in battle do we meet our fate,
they find their death in divination.

1918

*

High on Pieria's rocky ridges
the Muses first joined hands to dance
so that like bees the sightless singers
should pour Greek honey out for us.
The contours of a virginal forehead
breathed out a noble cooling wave
so that posterity should discover
the archipelago's tender graves.

Spring flies to tread the fields of Hellas,
Sappho has donned gay-colored shoes,
and the cicadas wield their hammers
to forge a ring, as the song goes.
The carpenter has raised a sturdy mansion,
fowls perish for the wedding feast,
a clumsy shoemaker has fashioned
all his five hides for dancing feet.

The lyric tortoise crawls out, sluggish
and clumsy on her toeless feet,
turns quietly in the Epirus sunlight
her golden belly to the heat.
But if you lure her and entrap her,
then turn her over as she sleeps—
in her dreams she foresees Terpander,
expecting those dry fingers' sweep.

The gelid well waters the oak trees,
grass rustles, head bare to the dew,
the wasps delight in the sweet lungwort.
You blessed isles, oh, where are you
where no stale, crumbly bread is eaten,

but only honey, wine, and milk,
where harsh toil does not dim the heavens
and the wheel turns, as soft as silk?

1919

We shall all meet again in Petersburg,
as if there we had buried the sun,
and we shall speak the blessed senseless word,
pronounce it there for the first time.
In the black velvet of the Soviet night,
the velvet of the cosmic void,
the blessed women's beloved eyes still sing
and immortelles still open wide.

The capital lies hunched like a fierce cat,
out on the bridge stands a patrol,
only a vicious car will hurtle past
through mist and make a cuckoo's call.
I can approach the sentries without fright,
I need no passport or password:
I shall be praying in the Soviet night,
praying for the blessed, senseless word.

I hear a faint theatrical commotion,
the whisper of a girlish "Ah"—
and a great cluster of immortal roses
is lying in the Cyprian's arms.
We warm ourselves by bonfires against boredom,
perhaps the centuries will pass,
and the beloved hands of blessed women
will gather up the fragile ash.

Somewhere there are the sweet choirs of *Orfeo*
and the familiar dark-brown eyes,
and down on the flowering rows of stalls the posters
like doves fall from the gallery.

So what then, if you wish, blow out our candles,
in the black velvet of the cosmic void
they sing, the blessed women's sudden shoulders,
but you'll not see the sun of night.

1920

*

Heaviness, tenderness—sisters—your marks are the same.
The wasps and the honey bees suck at the heavy rose.
Man dies, heat drains from the once warm sand,
and on a black bier they carry off yesterday's sun.

O, you tender nets and you heavy honeycombs,
easier to lift a stone than to speak your name!
Only one care is left me in the world:
a care that is golden, to shed the burden of time.

I drink the mutinous air like some dark water.
Time is turned up by the plow, and the rose was earth.
Slowly they eddy, the heavy, the tender roses,
roses of heaviness, tenderness, twofold wreath.

March 1920

When Psyche-life, following Persephone,
goes down to the shades in the half-forgotten trees,
a blind swallow flings itself against her feet
with Stygian tenderness and a branch still green.

A host of shades run out to meet her flight,
greeting their new friend with a keening note,
and gaze at her, and wring their feeble hands,
uncomprehending, full of fearful hope.

One holds a mirror, one a perfume flask—
the soul is a woman, trifles warm her heart—
and the bare wood filters their dry complaints,
transparent voices, like a fine small rain.

And in tender confusion, at a loss,
the soul can't recognize the transparent oaks,
breathes on a glass, reluctantly pays out
the copper coin for the misted ferry boat.

1920

*

I have forgotten the word I wanted to say.
The blind swallow will return to the hall of shades
on clipped wings to sport with transparent ones.
In unconsciousness the song of night is sung.

No sound of birds. No flower on the immortelles.
Transparent the manes of horses of the night.
In the dry river floats an empty shell.
Unconscious the word where the grasshoppers cry.

And gradually it grows, like a temple or tent.
Suddenly it will play the mad Antigone,
or like a dead swallow throw itself at the feet
with Stygian tenderness, a branch of green.

Oh, to bring back the shame of seeing fingers
and convex recognition's happiness!
I am so fearful of the Muses' keening,
of clangor, mist, and yawning emptiness.

But mortals have power to love and recognize,
for them sound too flows through the finger ends,
but I have forgotten what I want to say,
the bodiless thought will return to the hall of shades.

The transparent one still sings to no avail,
still swallow, Antigone, beloved girl . . .
but on the lips like black ice I feel
the memory of Stygian clangor burn.

November 1920

Take from my palms some sun to bring you joy
and take a little honey—so the bees
of cold Persephone commanded us.

No loosing of the boat that is not moored,
no hearing of the shadow shod in fur,
no overcoming fear in life's dense wood.

And kisses are all that's left us now,
kisses as hairy as the little bees
who perish if they fly the hive.

They rustle in transparent depths of night,
their home the thick woods on Taigetos' slopes,
their food is honeysuckle, mint, and time.

So for your joy receive my savage gift,
a dry and homely necklace of dead bees
that have transmuted honey into sun.

November 1920

Among the round of shades treading the tender meadow,
I came down here to dance, with a sonorous name . . .
but it all melted from me, just a shadow
of sound in my misted memory remained.

At first I placed the name with the seraphim
and kept my distance from the fragile body,
but just a few days gone, I merged with it
and lost myself in its beloved shadow.

And once again the tree sheds its wild apples,
and a secret image flashes on my sight,
and it blasphemes, curses itself and swallows
the burning coals that we call jealousy.

But happiness rolls by, like a golden hoop,
following the dictates of an alien will,
and you go chasing after fragile spring,
plowing the air with outstretched arms, and still

all is arranged in such a way that we
are held forever in the enchanted round.
The supple hills of the immaculate earth
lie tightly folded in their swathing bands.

1920

Because I hadn't the strength to hold on to your hands,
because I abandoned lips that are salty and loving,
I must wait for the day to return in the high city's darkness.
How I hate them, these ancient ramparts smelling of resin!

The men of Achaea equip a horse in the darkness,
and into its sides their sharp-toothed saws gnaw fiercely.
There's no way the blood's dry patter can be allayed,
there's no name for you, no sound, no mask, no molding.

How could I dare to have thought that you would return?
And why, when the time had come, did I desert you?
The darkness is not yet scattered, the cock has not sung,
the red-hot axe has not bitten into the timber.

Pitch has oozed out of the walls like transparent tears,
and the city can feel its ribs, their wooden structure,
but blood has welled up in the stairways and stormed the town,
and three times the Achaeans have seen it, the dream of temptation.

Where is lovely Troy, the king's and the maidens' house?
Priam's lofty aviary will be brought to nothing.
And arrows are raining down, a dry shower of wood,
and other arrows spring up from the earth like nut-twigs.

The sting of the final star without any pain is stilled,
and morning like a grey swallow will beat at the window,
and unhurried day, like an ox that wakes in the straw,
in the squares that are rough from too much sleep is stirring.

December 1920

from POEMS (1928)

*

I was washing at night out in the yard—
the heavens glowing with rough stars.
A star-beam like salt upon an axe,
the water barrel brimful and cold.

A padlock makes the gate secure,
and conscience gives sternness to the earth—
hard to find a standard anywhere
purer than the truth of new-made cloth.

A star melts in the barrel like salt,
and the ice-cold water is blacker still,
death is more pure, disaster saltier
and earth more truthful and more terrible.

1921

THE AGE

My age, my beast, where is the man
who can look into your eyes
and join together with his blood
the vertebrae of two centuries?
Blood-the-builder gushes out
of every earthly being's throat.
The parasite can only shake
on the threshold of new days.

A creature, while it clings to life,
must carry its backbone to the grave;
the spine within, invisible,
is tossed and tumbled by the waves.
And the earth's still infant age
seems the soft cartilage of a child;
they have brought the crown of life
like a lamb to the sacrifice.

To tear the age from captivity,
to begin the world anew,
the sections of uneven days
must be welded with a flute.
It is the age rocking the wave
with the grief of humankind
and in the grass the adder breathes
to the age's measure of gold.

And the new buds will swell again,
the sprouts of green splash forth,
but it is smashed to bits, your spine,
my age, pathetic, beautiful.
And with a smile that makes no sense

you look behind you, cruel and weak,
as a once agile beast looks back
at the tracks of its own feet.

1923

ONE WHO FINDS A HORSESHOE
a Pindaric fragment

We look to the forest and say:
A forest of ships, of masts,
the rose-colored pine trees
free of shaggy growth to the top
should go groaning into the storm,
lonely pines
in the furious treeless air, and under
the wind's salty heel the plumbline holds firm, made fast to the
    dancing deck.
And the seafarer
in his unbridled thirst for space,
dragging over damp furrows a geometer's fragile tools,
measures the pull of earth's heart
against the seas' rough face.

And inhaling the odor
of resinous tears that seep through the vessel's planking,
admiring the boards
jointed and shaped into bulkheads
not by that peaceable Bethlehem carpenter but by another—
the father of journeys, the friend of seamen—
we say:
They too stood on earth
as rough as a donkey's backbone,
tops forgetting their roots
on a noble mountain ridge,
and they rustled in freshwater showers
vainly pleading to heaven to change their illustrious burden
for a pinch of salt.

Where to begin?
Everything is cracking and rocking.
The air is shaking with similes.
No word is better than the next,
the earth buzzing with metaphor,
and the light two-wheelers
harnessed brightly to bird-flocks dense from the effort
break apart as they race
with the snorting lords of the stadium.

Thrice beloved is the man with a name in his song;
a song when adorned with a name
lives longer than the rest—
marked out from her friends by a headband
that cures her of swooning and over-strong odors—
the closeness of man
or the scent of the hide of a powerful beast
or simply the essence of savory crushed in the palm.

The air can be dark as water, all that lives in it swims like a fish,
pushing wide with its fins the sphere
that is full and elastic, just warm—
crystal, where wheels move and horses rear up,
damp black earth of Neaera, each night anew
with forks, tridents, mattocks, and plows.
The air is entangled, as dense as the earth—
you cannot get out, but it's hard to get in.

Like a green racket, a rustle runs through the trees;
children play at jacks with vertebrae of animals long dead.
Our age's fragile chronology is nearing an end.
Thank you for what was:
I myself was mistaken, lost my way, lost count.
The epoch rang like a golden ball,

empty, cast metal, supported by no one,
at every touch it replied "yes" or "no."
So a child replies:
"I'll give you an apple" or "I won't give you an apple."
And his face is molded on the voice that speaks those words.

The sound resounds though the cause of the sound has gone.
The horse lies in the dust and snorts in its foam,
but the sharp twist of its neck
still remembers the race with legs thrown wide—
not four,
but as many as the stones on the road
relayed in four shifts as
the blazing heat of the racer pushes from earth.

So
one who finds a horseshoe
blows the dust from it
and rubs it with wool till it shines,
then
hangs it up at the threshold,
allowing it to rest,
obliged no more to strike sparks from the flint.
Human lips that have no more to say
keep the shape of the last word spoken
and the hand keeps the feeling of weight
though the pitcher
                        lost half its water
                                  on the way back home.

What now I say is not said by me,
but dug out of the earth, like grains of petrified wheat.
Some
        on coins carve a lion,

others
      a head;
the different coins, the copper, the gold, and the bronze,
honored equally lie in the earth.
The age tried to gnaw them, leaving the print of its teeth.
Time is wearing me down like a coin
and my self is too little for me.

1923

SLATE PENCIL ODE

A mighty meeting—star with star,
the flinty road from the old song,
language of flint and tongue of air,
water with flint, horseshoe and ring.
On the soft-layered shale of clouds
a slate pencil's milky marks—
not the apprenticeship of worlds,
but sheepish ravings in the dark.

We stand in the dense night asleep,
warmed by this fleecy sheepish cap.
The spring, a warbling chain of speech,
into the mine runs gurgling back.
Here fear and dislocation write
with a white-lead crayon's gleam,
and here a rough draft comes to light
written by scholars of the stream.

Vertiginous cities of goats,
a mighty layering of flints;
and there is yet another ridge—
churches of sheep, their settlements!
The water teaches them, time wears,
the plumbline preaches what they know,
and the transparent woods of air
were sated with them long ago.

Like a dead drone beside the hive
bright day is swept away shamefaced.
And night the predator bears off
the burning chalk to feed the slate.
Oh, to wipe off the marks of day

from the iconoclastic board
and from the hand shake out the wraith
of visions, like a fledgling bird!

Fruit swelled. The grapes were growing ripe.
Day raged, as day will rage, and soon
came a sweet game of knucklebones
and the fierce collies' furs at noon.
Like garbage from the icy peaks
the hungry water flows and whirls—
the verso of the icons' green—
playing like a puppy with its tail.

And spiderlike it crawls on me,
where every meeting is moon-drenched.
On the astonished craggy steep
against the slate I hear chalk scratch.
Memory, is it you that speaks,
teaching, breaking the night to shards,
flinging chalks where the forest shakes,
tearing them from the beaks of birds?

For us, only the voice explains
all that was scratching, struggling there,
and we shall drag the dusty crayon
where the voice teaches us to steer.
I break the night, the burning chalk,
to trace a firm and short-lived line.
I change the din for arrows' talk,
change symmetry for angry cries.

Who am I? Not a man who builds,
no shipwright and no roofer I—
a double-dealer, double-souled,

champion of daylight, friend of night.
Happy the man who named the flint
a scholar of the flowing stream.
Happy the man who buckled the feet
of mountains on the solid ground.

And now I study the diary
scratched by summer on the slate,
language of flint and tongue of air,
a layering of dark and light,
and I would wish to put my hands
in the flint road of the old song
as in a flesh-wound, and so bind
water with flint, horseshoe, and ring.

1923

JANUARY 1, 1924

He who has kissed the crown of time's exhausted cranium
will feel a filial tenderness
remembering how time, outside the window,
in a wheat drift lay down to rest.
He who has lifted up his age's sickly eyelids—
two sleepy apples—he will hear
through all eternity the roaring of the rivers
of treacherous and empty years.

The tyrant-age has eyes like two great sleepy apples,
a handsome terracotta mouth—
but dying, he will fall against the hand of
a son who has said goodbye to youth.
I know, the breath of life, as each day passes, shortens,
and soon now they will put an end
to the song of the wrongs of terracotta
and seal the lips with molten tin.

O terracotta life! The age's gradual dying!
I fear you will be understood
only by those who wear the helpless smile of people
who have lost themselves in the dark wood.
What agony to seek a word that's vanished,
to lift the patient's lids, and then
with quicklime in the blood, to go by night to gather
herbs for an alien race of men.

The age . . . The quicklime in the son's sick blood grows thicker,
Moscow's asleep, a casket made of wood,
there is no place to run to from our age, the tyrant . . .
Snow smells of apples as of old.
I want to run away, to run far from my threshold.

Where shall I hide? The street is dark,
and like the salt they scatter on a cobbled causeway,
my conscience glistens, white on black.

A passenger like most, I've set off on my travels,
in meager furs, not going far,
by alleyways and low-slung eaves and starling-houses,
still wrestling to make fast the rug.
A street flicks idly past, and then another,
like apples the sleigh's runners crunch on ice,
the blanket loops put up a stiff resistance
and keep on slipping from my grasp.

Ringing like ironmongery, the night of winter
clatters along the Moscow streets.
A frozen fish, it knocks, and steam comes gushing
from pink cafés, like minnows' silver scales.
Again Moscow is Moscow. I say to her: "Good morning!
Don't lose your head; all is not lost.
As in the days of old, the brotherhood I honor
of the pike's justice and the frost."

The chemist's raspberry flagon flaming in the snowdrifts;
somewhere the clatter of an Underwood;
the cabbie's back and the deep snow—what more is needed?
You won't be touched. You won't be killed.
Winter-the-beautiful, and stars in the goat heavens
are scattered wide and burn like milk,
and like a horse's tail against the icy runners
the carriage blanket rubs and rings.

But the alleyways were smoking like oil lanterns,
gulping the raspberry ice and snow.
They hear in everything the Soviet sonatina,

remembering nineteen twenty. No,
could I surrender to the pillory of slander—
the ice still has an apple smell—
the vow I made the fourth estate, that wonder,
the solemn oath to which we wept?

Who else will you kill now? Who else will you make famous?
What will you make up now, what lies?
Rip out a key from the Underwood's gristly sinew,
you'll find the small bone of the pike.
And in the sick son's blood the quicklime dwindles,
and beatific laughter flows . . .
but our typewriter's simple sonatinas
are just those great sonatas' ghosts.

1924

*

I shall fling myself through the dark streets' gypsy encampment
in pursuit of a black sprung carriage, a branch of bird-cherry,
a hood of snow and the millrace's neverending din . . .

I only remember the misfiring of chestnut tresses
smoked over with bitterness, no, with the sharp admixture
of formic acid; they leave on the lips at such moments

the dryness of amber, the atmosphere seems to grow browner,
and rings around the eyes' pupils are arrayed in a lining
of lightness and all that I know of an apple-pink skin . . .

But runners of sleighs on the snow still kept on scraping,
the prickly stars looked down on the bast-work matting,
and the hooves of the horse beat time on the frozen piano.

And no light to be seen by the prickly lies of the stars,
and life will float by in the foam of an opera hood,
and no one will say: "from the dark streets' gypsy encampment" . . .

1925

LENINGRAD

I've come back to my city, which I know through my tears,
through a child's swollen glands, and deep down in my veins.

You've come back here, then swallow as fast as you can
the fish oil of Leningrad's riverside lamps.

Recognize then, and quickly, December's short days
where black sinister tar with egg-yellow is dyed.

Petersburg! I'm not ready to die quite so soon:
You have in your phone book the numbers I know.

Petersburg! I've addresses still fixed in my head
to find all the voices of those who are dead.

On a back stair, a black stair, I live, and the bell,
torn out by the roots, stabs my temple as well,

and I'll wait for those guests, those dear guests, all night long,
while the fetters of door-chains keep singing their song.

December 1930

With imperial power I was only connected through childhood,
being frightened by oysters, but daring to peep at the guardsmen ...
and I owe not a speck of my soul to that obsolete empire,
however I tortured myself to behave like the rest.

With stolid pomposity, scowling from under a beaver,
I never stood guard beneath the Egyptian bank portals,
and never, oh never, by the oily Neva did a gypsy,
to the rustle of banknotes, dance her dances for me.

Sensing trouble to come, from the roar of tumultuous action
I fled far away to the Black Sea, among the Nereids,
and from those belles dames—all of them European and tender—
what did I not suffer: embarrassment, injury, grief!

So why then, even today, does that city possess me,
my feelings and thoughts, as if by some ancient commandment,
the place that the fire and the cold have made even more brazen,
so empty, so youthful, self-satisfied, cursed?

Is it because as a child in a book I caught sight of
good Lady Godiva, her russet hair loosely cascading,
that I'm still repeating these words to myself *sotto voce:*
farewell then, Godiva ... I do not remember, Godiva.

January 1931

*

Help me, O Lord, to live through this long night:
I fear for life, I fear for her, your slave—
living in Petersburg's like living in a grave.

January 1931

*

We'll sit in the kitchen, you and I,
where the white paraffin smells sweet.

A round cob loaf and a sharp knife—
pump up the primus if you like.

Or gather together bits of string
to tie up the basket before dawn,

so we can set off to the station
where no one will track us down.

January 1931

For the noisy valor of future years,
for a lofty race of men,
I have lost my cup at the fathers' feast,
my honor, my cheerfulness.

The wolfhound century leaps on my back,
but I have no wolf in my blood,
oh, hide me deep and warm, like a cap
in the sleeve of Siberia's coat.

Let me see no coward, no sticky slime,
no wheel with bones and blood,
but silver foxes that shine all night
with a grace from before the flood.

Bear me off to the dark-flowing Yenisey
where pine trees stretch to the stars,
because I have no wolf in my blood,
and shall only be killed by my peers.

March 17–28, 1931

*

I drink to the asters of wartime, to all that they fling in my face,
to fur coats on toffs and to asthma, to Petersburg's petulant grace,

to the music of Saxony pinewoods, to the Champs-Elysées' fumes,
to Rolls-Royces loaded with roses, to the oils of Paris art-rooms.

I drink to the waters of Biscay, to the pitcher of Alpine cream,
to the pert red-haired English flappers, to the colonies with
    their quinine.

I drink to all this, but don't know yet which wine will give me
    more scope,
whether jovial Asti Spumante or the Château Neuf of the Pope.

April 11, 1931

Preserve my speech forever for its savor of sadness and smoke,
for the pitch of shared endurance, for the scrupulous tar of work,
as the water in Novgorod wells must be both black and sweet
so that in it the Christmas star is reflected with seven fins.

And for this, my father, my friend, and my rough helper, I—
the unacknowledged brother, the outcast of the family—
promise that I will build impenetrable log huts
so that in them the Tartar horde can drown princes in a tub.

If only I could be loved by the axeman's icy blocks,
as, aiming point-blank for death, people hammer home wooden stakes,
for this my whole life long I would wear an iron tunic
and find a great axe in the woods for a Petrine execution.

May 3, 1931

Not yet a patriarch, still years to go—
as yet my age is half respectable,
I'm still abused behind my back, I know,
in language that is fit for rowdy squabbles
on trams or buses, with no rhyme or reason:
"You so and so!" Well, I apologize,
but deep down there's no way I'll change my ways.

If you just think what ties you to the world,
you can't believe it, it's such nonsense :
the midnight key to someone else's place,
a silver penny sitting in your pocket,
a strip of celluloid for cops and robbers.

The telephone sees me rushing like a puppy
at every frantic ring. I catch a Polish
voice greeting me with its "Dziękuję, pani!"
or it's some interurban disapproval,
or a promise that will not be kept.

You wonder what you might acquire a taste for
among these firecrackers and these rockets:
You blow your top—everything stays the same,
the endless idleness and the confusion—
just try and get a light from one of them!

Sometimes I smirk, then timidly preen myself
and step out swinging a white-handled cane;
I listen to the sonatas in the alleys
and lick my lips at every hawker's tray,
then leaf through books in murky passageways—
I'm not alive, and all the same I live.

I'll go and see the sparrows, the reporters,
I'll go and see the street photographers
and in five minutes—just like a scoop of ice cream—
I'll see a reproduction of myself
standing beneath a lilac candy mountain.

And sometimes I'll go off on an errand
into the bowels of the steamy basements
where pure and honest Chinese folk with chopsticks
pick up their little balls of dough,
playing at cards with sharp-cut decks and sipping
vodka, like swallows on the Yangtze River.

I love the maneuvres of the screeching trams,
the Astrakhan caviar of the asphalt roadway
all covered with straw matting that looks like
the casing that protects a Chianti bottle,
and then the ostrich plumes that deck the carcass
of Leninist apartments as they rise.

I haunt the gorgeous caverns of the museums
where ogreish Rembrandts glare at me goggle-eyed
looking as glossy as Cordoba leather,
I stare entranced at Titian's horny mitres
and wonder at the motley Tintorettos.
the myriad vociferous parakeets.

And how I'd love to play the fool a bit,
to play the orator and speak out the truth,
to send spleen packing, send it to the devil—
to clutch at someone's hand—"Be good to me,"
I'd say to them, "we're going the same way . . ."

May–September 1931

Shove the papers in the drawer! Enough of gloom!
Today a gorgeous devil is in charge,
as if my head was shampooed to the roots
by my Parisian hairdresser François.

I'll bet my last kopeck I haven't died,
and, like a jockey, I can swear it's true
that I'm still vigorous enough to ride
on to the course and play a trick or two.

I don't forget that we now celebrate
thirty-one splendid years with flowering cherries
and that the worms of rain have come of age
and Moscow is all floating on its ferries.

Keep calm. Impatience is a luxury.
And softly, softly I shall begin to race:
I'll step on to the track unhurriedly,
for I have kept my distance in the chase.

June 7, 1931

*

Oh, how we love to fake and cheat,
how easily it is forgotten
that we are nearer death as children
than when we've reached maturity.

The child who hasn't slept enough
still sucks vexation from the bottle,
and I have no one left to sulk at,
I am alone on every path.

The beast will molt, and the fish plays
in the deep swooning of the water—
ah, must I witness the disorder
of people's passions, people's cares?

May 14, 1932

BATYUSHKOV

Like a flâneur with a magic cane,
tender Batyushkov lives at my place—
wanders down Zamostie lanes,
sniffs a rose, sings Zafna's praise.

Not believing for a moment that we
could be separated, I bowed to him:
I shake his brightly gloved cold hand
in an envious delirium.

He smiled at me. "Thank you," I said,
so shy I couldn't find the words:
No one commands such curves of sound,
never was there such speech of waves.

With oblique words he made us feel
the wealth and torments that we share—
the buzz of verse-making, brotherhood's bell
and the harmonies of pouring tears.

And the mourner of Tasso answered me:
"I am not yet used to eulogy;
I only cooled my tongue by chance
on the grape-flesh of poetry."

All right, raise your eyebrows in surprise,
city dweller and city dweller's friend—
like blood samples, from glass to glass
keep pouring your eternal dreams.

June 18, 1932

ARIOSTO

The cleverest man in Italy, untroubled,
suave Ariosto feels a little hoarse.
He revels in his catalogue of fish,
peppers the oceans with malicious babble.

Like a musician playing on ten cymbals,
he tirelessly snaps off the thread of tales,
not knowing his own way, he pulls all ways
his mixed-up story of chivalric scandals.

On the cicadas' tongue, a captivating mix—
Pushkinian sadness with southern conceit—
he catches Orlando in a web of deceit
and shudders, feeling utterly transfixed.

And to the sea he says: Roar without thought.
And to the maiden on the rock: Lie bare . . .
Tell us more tales, then, we can't get enough,
as long as blood flows in us and ears hear . . .

O town of lizards, where there's not a soul!
If only you could give us more like him,
Dreary Ferrara . . . Hurry, yet again,
as long as blood flows in us, tell us tales . . .

It's cold in Europe, dark in Italy.
Power is repulsive, like a barber's hands.
But he still lords it better, cunningly,
and out through the wide open window sends

a smile to the hill lambs, and to the monk
on donkeyback, and to the ducal troops,

silly from wine and garlic and the plague,
and to the child that sleeps among blue flies.

But I love his unbridled freedom, love
his foolish language, sweetly salted tongue,
and the enchanting clash of double sounds—
I fear to cut the pearl from the bivalve.

Suave Ariosto, who knows, an age will pass—
and into a single wide fraternal blue
we'll pour your azure and our own black sea.
. . . We too were there. And there we drank the mead . . .

May 4–6, 1933

*

Cold spring. Fearful Crimea with no grain.
All as in Wrangel's time—same guilty feeling.
Clods on the ground. Patches on tattered clothing.
The acid, biting smoke tastes just the same.

Still the same beautiful far-reaching steppe.
The trees, their buds just swelling up a little,
stand as they stood, you cannot help but pity
the almond in its silly Easter dress.

Nature, perplexed, doesn't know her own face.
Ukraine, Kuban cast their uncanny shadows,
and on the muffled earth the hungry peasants,
touching no rings, stand guard at their own gates.

Summer 1933
Moscow, after Crimea

*

Mozart in bird noise, Schubert on the water,
and Goethe, whistling on the winding road,
and Hamlet, with his timid steps still thoughtful,
took the crowd's pulse and trusted in the crowd.

Perhaps before the lips there was the whisper,
and leaves already whirled in treelessness,
and those for whom we seek new ways of writing
before our writing had acquired their face.

1933

The apartment—quiet as paper,
empty—has given up hope,
and you can hear how the water
goes gurgling through the pipe.

Property all in order,
phone crouched like a frog,
luggage that's crossed the border
just longing to be gone.

And the damned walls are flimsy,
there's nowhere left to run,
and for somebody, like an idiot,
I must fiddle a foolish tune.

Brasher than Komsomol chatter,
heartier than student chants,
I'll teach the axemen to twitter
sitting there on the school bench.

I peruse the ration booklets,
catch hempen words flying by,
and sing to the kolkhoz bosses
an ominous lullaby.

A kind of maker of pictures,
scraper of kolkhoz flax,
of blood and ink a mixer,
deserving this kind of task.

Some honest, treacherous dealer,
purged clean of feelings like salt,

provider for women and children,
will exterminate all the moths.

And so much unbearable malice
sings in each little whisper now
as if with a hammer Nekrasov
was knocking in nails anyhow.

So on the block let us together
begin after seventy years—
it's time for you, old and disheveled,
to clatter the boots you wear.

And instead of the Hippocrene fountain
a wave of old fear now flows
and breaks through the time-serving curtains
of this evil Moscow house.

November 1933

We live without touching the homeland beneath us—
The words that we speak can't be heard at ten meters.

When we manage a half-conversation,
We're obsessed by the Kremlin Caucasian.

His fingers are thick and as slimy as worms,
As solid as fifty-pound dumbbells his words.

His cockroachy whiskers keep smiling,
The tops of his boots are all shiny.

With their thin necks the bosses all swarm round their leader,
He just plays with the smirks of these weak semi-people.

They mew and they whinge and they whistle;
He alone does the bashing and whipping.

Like horseshoes he hammers out order on order
To their bellies, their eyebrows, their eyes and their foreheads.

Executions are what he loves best,
That Ossetian so broad in the chest.

November 1933

from the VORONEZH NOTEBOOKS (1935–1937)

*

I have to live, though twice now I have died,
and water drives this town out of its mind;
how beautiful it is, cheerful, strong-cheekboned, how
sweet is the fat earth's pressure on the plow;
how the spring turns the steppe to its advantage,
and sky, the wide sky, is your Buonarotti.

April 1935

BLACK EARTH

Too black, too much indulged, living in clover,
all little withers, all air, all charity,
all crumbling, all massing in a choir—
damp clods of soil, my land and liberty . . .

With early plowing it is black to blueness,
and unarmed labor here is glorified—
a thousand hills plowed open wide to say it—
circumference is not all circumscribed.

And yet the earth is blunder and obtuseness—
no swaying it, even on bended knee:
its rotting flute gives sharpness to the hearing,
its morning clarinet harrows the ear.

How sweet the fat earth's pressure on the plow,
how the spring turns the steppe to its advantage . . .
my greetings then, black earth: be strong, look out—
black eloquence of wordlessness in labor.

April 1935

What's the name of this street?
It's Mandelstam Street.
What a devil of a name!
Turn it this way or that,
it's twisted, not straight.

He wasn't too linear,
no lily, a sinner,
and that's why this street,
or rather, this pit,
is named after that man
called Mandelstam.

April 1935

*

After long-fingered Paganini
they all come running, the gypsy band—
a Czech, unchecked, a Polish fiddler,
and a Hungarian *chenchurá*.

You, lassie, classy, bold-as-brassy,
whose sound is wide as Yenisey,
comfort me with the tunes you play—
while on your Polish head you carry
Marina Mniszek's mound of hair,
your little fiddler's bow is wary.

Comfort me with the roan-brown Chopin,
the serious Brahms—no, not him here—
with Paris and its crazy fashion,
with carnivals, sweaty, and floury,
or with Vienna's youthful cheer—

flighty, in its conductors' tails,
in Danube fireworks, racecourse rails,
pouring out like intoxication
a waltz that whirls from grave to cradle.

So till the aorta bursts, play on
with that cat's head stuck in your mouth!
There were three devils, you're the fourth,
the last, a gorgeous devil in bloom.

April 5–June 18, 1935

*

We are still full of life up to the brim,
they still stroll through the cities of the Union,
the blouses and the dresses China-trimmed,
with palmate papilionaceous material.

The number one clipping machine still grasps
the chestnut-hued backhanders it can get;
and thickly-rooted reasonable locks
still flutter to the gleaming serviette.

There are still swifts and swallows in the sky,
no comet has driven us off the rails,
and violet-colored ink sensibly writes
and bears its load of stars and its long tail.

May 25, 1935

*

Yes, lying in the earth, my lips are moving,
but what I say, each child will learn by heart:

on Red Square the earth is at its roundest,
its voluntary slope more firmly set,

on Red Square the earth is at its roundest,
its slope is unexpectedly unfurled,

dropping away, down to the distant rice fields,
as long as slaves are living in the world.

May 1935

I

On this river, the Kama, how dark fills the eyes
when the cities kneel down on the oak of their knees.

Beard to beard, in a gossamer tunic, the firs
look young in the water, they run and they burn.

With a hundred and four sturdy oar blades, the stream
bore us up, bore us down to Kazan and Cherdyn.

There I sailed on the river, the window blind shut,
the window blind shut, and a fire in my head.

And by me my wife didn't sleep for five nights,
didn't sleep for five nights with three guards at her side.

II

Departing, I scanned the coniferous east,
while a buoy took the weight of the Kama in spate.

And I'd love to exfoliate mountains and fire,
but barely have time now to plant it with firs.

And I'd love to take root, understand if you can,
in the longstanding Urals, long peopled by man.

And I'd love to be able to save and to hold
this insane level space in the tails of my coat.

May 1935

*

Robbing me of the seas, a springboard and a sky,
forcing my foot to press the solid earth,
what use was that to you? With all your strategy
you could not take from me the lips that stir.

May 1935

STANZAS

1

I am not going to waste my soul's last penny
on the young creatures of the hothouse brood,
but, like a solitary in the collective,
I step into the world—where men are good.
I love the folds of the Red Army greatcoat—
down to the ground, its sleeves smooth and unpleated,
its cut resembling clouds over the Volga,
so that it swells out on the chest and back,
lying there freely, holding nothing over,
and then in summer rolls up like a sack.

2

A cursed seam, a crazy undertaking
divided us. And now, just understand:
I have to live, breathing and Bolshevizing,
and once again, even in the hour of dying,
to be and play some more with my own kind.

3

Just think how that time in full-scale confusion
I thrashed about in peaceful Cherdyn, where
you scent the Ob and the Tobol's profusion:
I didn't see the spiteful rams stop fighting,
like a young cock in summer's twilight glare—
the grub, the mugs, the you-know-what, the lying—
shrugged off the slurs. A jump.
                              And I'm all there.

4

And you, Moscow, my sister, light as grass
when from the aeroplane you meet your brother
before the first tram clangs to let it pass:
You're softer than the sea and more befuddled
than salad made of wood and milk and glass . . .

5

My country talked with me, at once indulging
and scolding me, not reading all I write,
but still it noticed how I had grown stronger
witnessing life, and like a lens in sunbeams
made me flare up, a little guiding light.

6

I have to live, breathing and Bolshevizing,
and work on language, stubborn, not alone.
Way north, I hear the Soviet engines grinding,
I see the German brothers' necks and know
how the bloodthirsty gardener fills his leisure
playing with Lorelei's sweet lilac comb.

7

I've not been robbbed, neither have I been broken,
but simply weighed down with a heavy burden . . .
my strings are stretched tight like the Tale of Igor,
asphyxia is gone, and in my voice
the earth resounds—the weapon of all weapons,
the black earth's million hectares, dryly moist!

May–July 1935

Can you praise a woman who's dead?
All strength and alienation . . .
Her alien-loving power has led
to a tomb that is fiery, violent.

And the firm swallows of her brows
flew from her grave and told me
they had rested beneath the snows
of her funeral bed in Stockholm.

Your tribe prized the violin
of your ancestor, shapely and graceful,
and you'd open wide scarlet lips
and laugh, both Italian and Russian.

I cherish your memory's load,
wild thing, little bear, and Mignon—
but the mill-wheels sleep under snow
and the postman's horn is frozen.

June 3, 1935–December 14, 1936

*

A wave runs on, wave breaking a wave's back,
throwing itself at the moon in captive grief,
and janissary-like, the youthful deep,
the unabating capital of waves,
blind, hurls itself and digs a trench in sand.

But through the gloomy flakiness of air
the turrets of an unbuilt wall are glimpsed
and from the foaming stairs fall soldiers
of jealous sultans—torn and dashed to drops—
and the cold eunuchs bring the poison cups.

July 1935

*

From past the houses and the trees,
longer than freight trains' harmonies,
hoot while I work and strengthen me,
Sadko of gardens and factories.

Hoot, guardian, and sweetly breathe,
like Sadko of Novgorod the free
deep in the seething cobalt sea,
keep hooting through the centuries,
siren of Soviet history.

December 6–9, 1936

*

My goldfinch, I'll toss back my head—
let's look at the world, you and I:
a wintry day, prickly as stubble,
is it just as rough on your eye?

Tail like a boat, black and gold plumage,
dipped in paint from the beak down—
are you aware, my little goldfinch,
what a goldfinch dandy you are?

What air there is on his forehead:
black and red, yellow and white!—
he keeps a sharp lookout both ways,
won't look now, he's flown out of sight.

December 1936

*

The pine grove's law speaks in one voice:
viols' and harps' united noise.
The trunks are bare, they bend and bow,
but still the harps and viols grow
as if Aeolus had begun
to twist trunks into harps, and then
abandoned it, to spare the roots,
to spare the trunk, the strong young shoots,
waking the viols and the harps
in the brown darkness of the bark.

December 16–18, 1936

*

The idol sits unmoved within the mountain
in his unbounded, rounded, guarded chambers,
while from his neck the grease of jewels drips,
protecting dreams that ebb and flow.

When he was a boy, a peacock was his playmate,
they fed him on a rainbow of the Indies
and gave him milk out of rose-colored clay
and never spared the cochineal.

Lulled into sleep the bone is knitted up,
the knees, the hands, the shoulders all seem human.
He smiles with his own quietest of smiles,
thinking with bone and feeling with his forehead,
attempting to recall his human features.

December 1936

Through my cabin windowpane
the distant line of caravans . . .
from the frost and from the warmth
the river seems not far away.
And the woods—are those trees pines?

No, not pines, but lily lines!—
and that birch tree standing there,
I'll never say just what it is:
just the prose of skylit ink
illegible and light as air . . .

December 26, 1936

*

Day is a kind of greenhorn now—
I can't make it out,
and the sea barriers stare at me
in anchors and in cloud.

Quiet, quiet on the bleached water
the warships' slow advance,
and the narrow slits of the channels
lie black beneath the ice.

December 28, 1936

*

I'll marvel at the world, the snows,
and the children yet a while,
but with a true, authentic-as-the-road,
free, disobedient smile.

December 1936

*

Yeast of the world, dear yeast of time:
sounds and tears and works of men—
drumbeats like the falling rain
of calamity to come,
sounds that now no longer sound,
out of what ore can they be mined?

In poverty-stricken memory
you first sense blind concavities
filled with water copper-green—
and you walk where they have been,
to your own self unloved, untried—
a blind man and a blind man's guide . . .

January 12–18, 1937

*

You've not died yet, and still you're not alone
as long as with your poor beloved
you revel in the plains, their cold
magnificence, the mist, the blizzard.

In lovely want, luxurious poverty
you can live peaceful, live consoled—
blessed be every night and every day,
blessed the blameless, sweet-voiced toil.

Unhappy the man who like his shadow
fears the barking dogs, the scything wind,
and pitiful who half alive
begs coppers from a shadow's hand.

January 15–16, 1937

*

Alone, I look into the frost's face:
I come from nowhere, it is going nowhere,
and still the breathing miracle of the plain
is ironed flat, pleated without a wrinkle.

And in starched poverty the sun
screws up his eyes, tranquil and comforted . . .
The unnumbered forests are still much the same . . .
Eyes crunch the snow, like innocent white bread.

January 16, 1937

*

What can we do with the deadness of the plains,
the long-drawn hunger of their miracle?
For what we deem to be their openness
we too can see as we drift off to sleep—
and still the question grows: whither and whence
are they? and is he not crawling over them
slowly, the one of whom we cry in sleep,
the Judas of the peoples still to come?

January 16, 1937

Oh, this slow spaciousness, so short of breath!
I've had more than I can take—the sky
flung open wide, restored, refreshed—
Oh, for a bandage on my eyes!

I could have better borne the layered sand
on Kama's battlemented margin:
I should have hung on to her modest sleeve,
her deeps, her eddies, and her edges.

I should have teamed with her for minutes, eons,
still envious of her lurking rapids,
I should have listened to the woody rings
beneath the bark, fibrous and sappy . . .

January 16, 1937

*

How womanly silver will still burn
having fought off oxide and alloys,
and quiet work lays silver on
the iron plow, the poet's voice.

January 1937

*

Now I am in a spider's web of light—
web of dark hair, web of light brown tresses—
the people need bright light and pale blue air,
they need bread and they need the snow of Elbruz.

There's no one I can get advice from here,
and I shall hardly seek it out unaided—
for such transparent stones, such stones that weep
are not found in the Urals or Crimea.

The people need secretly-homely verse
so they can be constantly awaking
and in the linen-curling, chestnut waves
of its cool breathing still be washing . . .

January 19, 1937

*

I hear the January ice,
whispering beneath the bridges,
and I remember other skies,
and over heads hops' brightness.

From stale staircases and squares,
palaces all walls and angles,
his lips eaten thin by care,
Dante sang with all the more
power of his Florence circle.

So my shadow feasts its eyes
on that coarse-grained northern granite,
seeing the axeman's blocks by night
where the daylight painted mansions,

or my shadow shifts and sighs,
yawns a bit with you from habit,

or it joins the noisy crowd,
seeking warmth in wine or sky,

feeding bread, tasteless and dry,
to the unrelenting swans.

January 22, 1937

Like Rembrandt, martyr of the chiaroscuro,
I have gone deep into the days of silence,
but the sharp outline of my burning rib
is not protected by that noble warrior
nor by those guards who sleep beneath the storm.

Can you forgive me, my resplendent brother,
master and father of the black-green shadow?—
yet the eye open on the falcon's feather
and the warm caskets of the midnight harem
do not do good, but without goodness trouble
the tribe made restless by the twilight's furs.

February 8, 1937

*

Armed with the eyesight of thin-waisted wasps
that suck at the earth's axis, the earth's axis,
I sense it all, all that I ever saw,
and vainly, word for word, try to recall it . . .

I make no pictures, neither do I sing
nor draw the black-voiced bow across the string:
I only suck on life, and love to envy
the wasps, so potent and so sly.

Oh, if I too could one day be impelled
by summer's heat and by the air's sharp practice
to feel, as I avoided sleep and death,
earth's axis, yes, to penetrate earth's axis . . .

February 8, 1937

*

I sing when my throat is moist and my soul is dry,
and my eyes are damp, and conscience tells no lies.
Is the wine good? And are the fur coats good?
Good the commotion of Colchis in the blood?
The chest is drawn tight, without language, quiet:
and now not I am singing but my breath—
my hearing sheathed in mountains, my head deaf.

A generous song is to itself high praise,
pleasure to friends and pitch to enemies.

A one-eyed song, growing up out of moss,
the one-voiced bounty of the hunter's life,
sung in the saddle or on mountaintops,
holding the breath freely and openly,
with just one honest goal, to bring the bride
and groom to the wedding, safely, angrily . . .

February 8, 1937

*

Rendings of rounded bays and gravel and deep blueness,
and the slow sail continuing in cloud,
I have been taken from you, I hardly knew you:
Longer than organ fugues, the grass of seas false-haired,
bitter, and smells of enduring lies—
an iron tenderness intoxicates the mind
and rust gnaws weakly at the sloping shoreline . . . Why then
do I feel underneath my head a different sand?
You, Ural of the throat, the Volga lands' broad shoulders,
or this flat territory—these are my only rights,
and I must breathe them in to fill my lungs.

February 8, 1937

*

I shall say it in draft, in a whisper—
since the time has not come yet:
The games of nonchalant heaven
are won only by living and sweat.

And under the temporary sky
of purgatory we may forget
that this happy sky-reservoir
is our nomad's home till death.

March 9, 1937

*

Do not compare: what lives is incomparable.
I felt a a kind of tender fear
as I took on the plains' equality
and the wide sky became my malady.

I summoned the air, my serving man,
expected from him services or news,
made ready to set out, sail on the arc
of expeditions that could never start.

Where I have most sky I am glad to roam,
and a bright sadness will not let me leave
Voronezh and its adolescent hills
for the clear human hills of Tuscany.

March 16, 1937

*

Oh, how I wish that I
not seen by anyone
could fly after the ray
where the I is quite gone.

And you shine in that ring—
no happiness but that—
as from the stars you learn
the meaning of the light.

But when I whisper here
to you I want to say
that with this whisper I
give you, child, to the ray.

It is only a ray
and it is only light
when whispering gives it power
and lisping is delight.

March 27, 1937

*

The potters exalt the blue island—
Crete the green. Their gift is baked in
the echoing earth. Hear the thrashing
of the dolphins' underground fins.

This sea is there for the taking
in the clay made glad by the glaze,
and the ice-cold strength of the vessel
is split between sea and eyes.

Give me back what is mine, blue island,
winged Crete, give me back my task,
and nourish the glazed earthen vessel
at the goddess's flowing breast.

This is and was sung, and was blue
long before Odysseus came,
before the time when the food
and drink were called "mine" and "thine."

Grow well again, radiate,
star of the ox-eyed sky,
and the flying fish is just chance,
and the water that answers "Aye."

March 1937

*

I lift this green to my lips,
lift the leaves, their sticky oath,
the oath-breaking earth that gives
birth to poplars, maples, oaks.

See me grow blind and strong
serving humble roots, and say:
Is the park's stentorian song
not too sumptuous for the eye?

And toads, quicksilver beads,
join voices to stitch a sphere,
and branches grow from twigs,
a milky fiction from steam.

April 30, 1937

*

There are women akin to the damp earth,
their every step a deep sobbing,
their calling to accompany the risen
and be first to welcome the dead.
To ask tenderness of them is a crime
and to part with them impossible.
Today angel, tomorrow graveyard worm,
and the next day no more than an outline . . .
what was once just a step no more possible . . .
Flowers undying. Sky incorruptible.
And all that's to come just a promise.

May 4, 1937

PROSE

from THE NOISE OF THE TIMES

CHILDHOOD IMPERIALISM

Round and round the equestrian statue of Nicholas I opposite the State Assembly, never deviating, marched a grenadier mossy with age, his head crammed winter and summer alike into a shaggy sheepskin cap. His headgear looked like a mitre and was almost the size of a whole sheep.

We children would get into conversation with this decrepit sentry. He disappointed us by not being a veteran of 1812, as we had thought. But he told us about the "old guys," survivors of Nicholas's guards, of whom only five or six remained in the entire company.

The entry to the Summer Garden from the Embankment with its gates and chapel and the one opposite the Engineers' Palace were guarded by bemedalled sergeant majors, who judged whether people were properly dressed, driving away wearers of Russian boots, and repulsing folk in peaked caps and vulgar outfits. The manners of children in the Summer Garden were very formal. After whispering with a nanny or governess, some barelegged child would come up to your bench and with a little bow or curtsy squeak out, "Little girl (or little boy, such were the official forms of address) would you like to play at golden gate (or hide-and-seek)?"

You can imagine what sort of fun the game was after such an opening. I never played, and this way of making friends seemed unnatural to me.

It so happened that my early Petersburg childhood took place under the sign of the most authentic militarism, and to be fair, this was not my fault, but the fault of my nanny and of the Petersburg streets in those days.

We used to go for walks along the deserted tracts of Bolshaya Morskaya Street near the red Lutheran kirk and the woodblock pavements on the banks of the Moyka.

Here, on the green unused roadway, the marines were drilled, and the canal water shook from the noise of brassy kettledrums and bass drums.

I liked the physique of these men, all of them taller than average. The nursemaids completely shared my tastes. So we marveled at one sailor— "Black Moustache"—and came specially to look at him; once we had found him, we didn't take our eyes off him as long as the drill lasted. I can say now without a moment's hesitation that at the age of seven or eight the whole mass of Petersburg, its granite and woodpaved quarters, all the tender heart of the city with the expanse of squares, the leafy gardens, the islands of statues, the caryatids of the Hermitage and the mysterious Millionnaya Street where there were no strollers and just one single dairy shop squeezed in amidst a mass of marble, and above all the Arch of the General Staff, Senate Square, and Dutch Petersburg—all this was for me something sacred and festive.

I don't know how the imagination of young Romans peopled their Capitoline, but I peopled these squares and strongholds with some kind of impossible, ideal, universal parade.

Typically, I didn't believe for one moment in the Kazan Cathedral, in spite of the tobacco-brown gloom of its vaults and its tattered forest of banners.

This too was an unusual place, but more of that later. The stone horseshoe of the colonnade and the broad pavement with its little guard chains were preordained for an uprising, and in my imagination this place was interesting and meaningful on a par with the Mayday parade on the Field of Mars. —What will the weather be like? Will it be put off? Will it even take place this year? . . . But already the planks and boards have been laid down along the Summer Canal, already the carpenters are hammering away on the Field of Mars; already the stands tower like mountains, already the dust is rising from the mock attacks, and the foot soldiers drawn up in ultrastraight lines are waving their little flags. It took about three days to construct this stand. Such speed seemed magical to me, and the size of it weighed on me like a Coliseum. Every day I came to look at the building work, admired the smoothness of the operations, scrambled up ladders, feeling myself on a stage, a participant in the next day's brilliant ceremony, and I envied even the planks that would no doubt witness the attack.

All the pandemonium of a hundred military bands, the field bristling with bayonets, the parallel strips of infantry and cavalry, as if it was not regiments mustered there but rows of buckwheat, rye, oats, and barley. And the secret movement between regiments inside the clearings in the ranks! And then the silver trumpets and horns, the babel of shouts, kettledrums, bass drums . . . And the sight of a cavalry charge!

I always had the impression that in Petersburg something very grandiose and ceremonial was bound to take place.

I was in raptures when the lampposts were draped in black crepe and hung with black ribbons for the funeral of a Crown prince. The mounting of the guard at the Alexander Column, the obsequies of generals, the "progresses," such were my daily entertainments.

"Progresses" was the name given in those days to the processions of the tsar and his family through the streets. I took good care to find out all about them. On a given day the palace officials would come creeping out of the Anichkov Palace like ginger-whiskered cockroaches: "Nothing to see, ladies and gentlemen. Move along please. Be so good . . ." But the janitors were already scattering yellow sand from their wooden shovels, the constables' whiskers had been dyed, and there were policemen strewn like peas along Kolonnaya or Konyushennaya Street.

It amused me to pester the police with my questions—Who will be going past? And when?—questions they never dared answer. I must admit though that the glimpse of a carriage with a coat-of-arms and golden birds on the lamps or of an English sleigh with hooded trotting horses never failed to disappoint me.

The Petersburg streets gave me an appetite for grand spectacle, and the very architecture of the city inspired me with a kind of childish imperialism. I raved about the cavalry armor and the Roman helmets of the horse guards and about the silver trumpets of the Preobrazhensky band; after the Mayday parade what I liked best was the horse guards' regimental ceremony on Annunciation Day.

I remember too the launching of the battleship *Oslyabya*, the great sea monster crawling out onto the water, the cranes and the ribs of the slipway.

All this accumulation of militarism, with even a touch of police aesthetic, was well suited to the son of some company commander with the right family traditions, but sat very badly with the cooking fumes of a petty bourgeois apartment, the paternal office smelling of leather, sheep skins and calf hides, and the Jewish business conversations.

UPRISINGS AND MADEMOISELLES

The days of student uprisings by the Kazan Cathedral were always known in advance. Every household had its student informant. The way it turned out, these uprisings were observed, from a respectful distance it's true, by a sizeable audience: children with their nannies, mamas, and aunties who hadn't been able to stop their insurgents from venturing forth, old civil servants, and all manner of idlers. On the day appointed for the uprising, the sidewalks of Nevsky Prospect would be heaving with a dense body of spectators all the way from Sadovaya Street to the Anichkov Bridge. This great mob was afraid to approach the Kazan Cathedral. The police were concealed in courtyards such as that belonging to St. Catherine's Church. Kazan Square was relatively free of people, just small groups of students or genuine workers strolling about, with the latter being pointed out by onlookers. Suddenly from Kazan Square would come a prolonged howl, getting louder and louder, something that sounded like "ooo" or "yyy," turning into a fierce bellow, coming closer and closer. Then the spectators would make a dash for it, and horses would burst into the crowd. A shout of "Cossacks! Cossacks!" would flash out, quicker even than the Cossacks themselves. The actual "uprising" would be rounded up and taken off to the Mikhailovsky Manege, and Nevsky Prospect would be emptied, as if a broom had swept it clean.

My first vividly conscious impression was of somber crowds of people on the streets. I was just three years old. It was 1894, and I had been brought from Pavlovsk into Petersburg to see the funeral of Alexander III. We had rented a room on the fourth floor of a furnished house on Nevsky

Prospect somewhere opposite Nikolaevskaya Street. Already the previous evening I climbed up on the windowsill and saw the street black with people; I asked, "When are they coming?" and they said "Tomorrow." What struck me most was that all these crowds of people were spending the night on the street. Even death first appeared to me in a completely unnatural form, grandiose and pompous. One day I was walking with my nanny and my mother along Moyka Street past the chocolate-colored building of the Italian Embassy. All of a sudden the embassy doors were flung open and anyone could enter; there was a smell of resin, incense, and something pleasantly sweet. Black velvet muffled the entrance and the walls, which were adorned with silver and tropical plants; high above the floor lay the embalmed body of the Italian ambassador. What had all that to do with me? I don't know, but the impressions were clear and powerful, and even today I treasure them.

The everyday life of the city was barren and monotonous. About five o'clock each day there was a promenade on Bolshaya Morskaya Street, from Gorokhovaya Street to the Arch of the General Staff Building. All the idle and grand people of the city moved slowly up and down the sidewalks, bowing and smiling to one another: With the clashing of spurs and the sounds of French and English, it was a living exhibition of the English Emporium and the Jockey Club. This was where the *bonnes* and the governesses, young Frenchwomen, brought the children, sighing as they compared it with the Champs Elysées.

I had so many mademoiselles hired for me that all their features merged into one blurred, common portrait. As far as I could see, their little rhymes, copybooks, readers, and conjugations had made children of them all. At the heart of the distorted worldview peddled by the readers stood the figure of the great Emperor, Napoleon, and the war of 1812, followed by Joan of Arc (though as it happened one of the Swiss girls was a Calvinist), and however hard I tried, eager pupil that I was, to extract some idea of France from them, I discovered only that it was a beautiful country. The French girls prized the art of speaking quickly and volubly, and the Swiss girls the knowledge of songs, chief among which was "*Malbrouk s'en va-t-en guerre*." These poor girls were imbued with the cult of great men: Hugo, Lamartine, Napoleon, Molière... On Sundays they were let out to Mass, but they weren't allowed any acquaintances.

A scene somewhere in the Ile de France: wine barrels, white roads, poplar trees—a winegrower has gone off with his daughters to visit their grandmother in Rouen. He gets back to find the *scellés* in place, the wine presses with their fumes all sealed up, sealing wax on the doors and cellars. The manager has been caught trying to conceal some flasks of new wine from the exciseman. The family is ruined, forced to pay a huge fine, and thus the stern laws of France make me the present of a nanny.

But what had I to do with the guards' ceremonies, the monotonous beauty of the massed infantry and the horses, the stony-faced battalions moving with muffled tread over the granite and marble greyness of Millionnaya Street?

The whole harmonious image of Petersburg was just a dream, a brilliant cover thrown over the abyss, and all around stretched Judaic chaos, not a motherland, not a hearth, not a home, but a real chaos, an obscure, womblike world from which I had emerged, which I feared, and which I dimly sensed and fled, always fled.

The Judaic chaos made its presence felt through all the cracks in the stone-built Petersburg apartment by the threat of collapse, by the cap worn indoors by some visitor from the provinces, by the spiky letters of the unread books of Genesis lying in the dust on the bottom shelf of the bookcase below Goethe and Schiller, or by the scraps of black and yellow ritual.

The strong, ruddy Russian year rolled by according to the calendar, with its painted eggs, Christmas trees, steel skates from Finland, December, Shrovetide cabs, and *dachas*. But there was a specter lurking among them: the New Year in September and the strange cheerless feast days with savage names that grated on the ear: Rosh Hashanah, Yom Kippur.

THE BOOKCASE

Just as a drop of musk can permeate a whole house, so the slightest hint of Judaism can permeate a whole life. What a pervasive odor it is! How could I not notice that genuine Jewish houses do not smell the same as Aryan ones? And it's not just the kitchen that smells, but the people, the objects, the clothing. Even today I can remember how this cloying Jewish smell enveloped me in the wooden house on Klyuchevaya Street in German Riga where my grandparents lived. And indeed my father's office at home was already different from the granite paradise of my elegant walks; it led into another world, whose heterogeneous decor and collection of objects were inextricably knotted together in my mind. First of all there was the handmade oak armchair with its carving of a balalaika and a gauntlet and on its curved back the motto: "Slowly but surely"—a nod to the pseudo-Russian style of Alexander III's reign; then came the Turkish divan, crammed with ledgers whose cigarette-paper pages were covered with the crabbed Gothic script of German business letters. At first I thought that my father's work consisted in printing his own cigarette-paper letters by turning the handle of the copying machine. To this day the true smell of hard labor is for me that smell of tanned leather that gets everywhere—and the complete calf hides scattered over the floor, the little protrusions of puffy chamois leather like living fingers, all this together with the small businessman's desk and its little marble calendar floats in a haze of tobacco smoke spiced with the smell of leather. But in this stuffy office decor there was a little glass-fronted bookcase, draped in green taffeta. And it's this storehouse of books that I want to write about. The bookcase of early childhood keeps you company all through life. The arrangement of the shelves, the choice of books, the color of the bindings are experienced as the arrangement, height, and color of world literature itself. Yes, those books that were not in that first bookcase will never make it into world literature or indeed into the world order. Like it or not, in the first bookcase every book is a classic; not one volume can be thrown away.

It was not by chance that this strange little library was laid down over the years in a kind of geological stratification. The paternal and maternal strata did not mingle, but remained distinct, and in cross-section this little bookcase was the history of the spiritual tensions of a whole race and its transfusions of alien blood.

I remember the bottom shelf as always chaotic: the books did not stand spine to spine but lay like ruins: russet-colored Pentateuchs with torn covers, a Russian history of the Jews, written in the clumsy, tentative language of a a Russian-speaking Talmudist. The Judaic chaos was reduced to dust here. This is where my Ancient Hebrew alphabet quickly came to rest, never learned by me. In a fit of national repentance they had hired a real Hebrew teacher for me. He would arrive from his place on Torgovaya Street and teach me without taking his hat off, which made me feel uncomfortable. His educated Russian speech sounded forced. The Hebrew alphabet had pictures representing in a variety of positions—with a cat, a book, a bucket, a watering can—one and the same boy in a cap with a very sad, grownup face. I did not recognize myself in this boy and rebelled with all my being against the book and its lessons. There was one thing about this teacher that was remarkable, even if it sounded unnatural—a feeling of Jewish national pride. He spoke about the Jews as the French girls had spoken about Hugo and Napoleon. But I knew that he concealed his pride once he was out in the street, and consequently I didn't believe him.

Above the Jewish ruins began the organized book world, the Germans: Schiller, Goethe, Kerner, Shakespeare in German—old Leipzig and Tübingen editions, dumpy little fellows in claret-colored embossed covers, with small print designed for strong young eyes and hazy engravings in a somewhat antique style: women with their hair down wringing their hands, a lamp drawn to look like an oil lamp, horsemen with high foreheads and vignettes of bunches of grapes. This was my autodidact father breaking out of the thickets of the Talmud into the Germanic world.

Higher still were my mother's Russian books—Pushkin in the 1876 Isakov edition. I still think this is a splendid edition; I like it better than the Academy edition. There is nothing superfluous in it, the lines of type are shapely, the columns of verse flow freely like soldiers in mobile detachments, and ahead of them, like leaders, march the precise, sensible years, up to and including 1837. And Pushkin's color? All colors are random—What color can you give to the babble of speech? Oh, Rimbaud and his idiotic alphabet of colors! . . .

My Isakov Pushkin wore a vestment of no special color, a high-school calico binding, a faded blackish-brown vestment with a touch of sandy earth; it feared neither stains, nor ink, nor fire, nor kerosene. Over a quarter of a century, the sandy black vestment had lovingly absorbed everything—I can distinctly feel the spiritual, dinner-table beauty, the almost physical charm of my mother's Pushkin. It bears an inscription in red ink: "Awarded to a pupil of the 3rd form for hard work." This Isakov Pushkin tells a story of idealistic teachers of both sexes with the flush of consumption on their cheeks and holes in their shoes: Vilnius in the 1880s. The word "intellectual" was spoken with pride by my mother and especially by my grandmother. Lermontov had a greenish-blue binding, somewhat military in appearance—not for nothing was he a hussar. He never seemed to me a brother or a relative of Pushkin. Whereas Goethe and Shakespeare I saw as twins. In Lermontov's case though I sensed something alien and consciously set it apart. After 1837 blood and verse flowed differently.

And what of Turgenev and Dostoevsky? They were supplements to a newspaper, *Niva*. They looked alike, just like brothers: cardboard covers bound in leather. A ban covered Dostoevsky like a gravestone; he was seen as "difficult." Turgenev was permitted and wide open with his Baden-Baden, his *Spring Waters*, and his leisurely conversations. But I knew that the peaceful life of Turgenev's novels had gone and was nowhere to be found.

Grass on the streets of Petersburg—the first shoots of a virgin forest that will cover the sites of our modern cities. This vivid, tender green, remarkable for its freshness, belongs to a new vibrant nature. Petersburg is indeed the most advanced city in the world. The march of modernity, its speed, is not measured by underground trains or by skyscrapers, but by the cheery grass poking up through the stones of the city.

Our blood, our music, our state, all this is perpetuated in the tender existence of a new nature, nature-as-Psyche. In this realm of the spirit without humanity every tree will be a dryad, and every phenomenon will speak of its own metamorphosis.

Put a stop to this? Why should we? Who will stop the sun as it hastens with its team of sparrows back to its father's house, gripped by the desire of homecoming? Is it not better to greet it with praise than try and wheedle a present out of it?

> Little he ever understood,
> He had a child's timidity,
> His frame was weak, his livelihood
> Hung upon strangers' charity . . .

We can thank the "strangers" for their touching concern, their tender care for the old world, which is "not of this world" and is entirely devoted to expectation and preparation for the coming metamorphosis:

> *Cum subit illius tristissima noctis imago,*
> *Quae mihi supremum tempus in urbe fuit,*
> *Cum repeto noctem, qua tot mihi cara reliquit,*
> *Labiter ex oculis nunc quoque gutta meis.*

[When I see the terrible image of that night which marked my departure from Rome, when I recall that night which took away so much that was dear to me, even today tears flow from my eyes. (Ovid, *Tristia*.) See "Tristia" on page 29.]

Yes, the old world is "not of this world," but it is more alive than ever. Culture has become a church. There has been a separation of culture-as-church and the state. Worldly life no longer concerns us; we have not food but a sacrament, not a room but a cell, not clothing but raiment. At last we have found an inner freedom, a true inward cheer. We drink water from clay vessels like wine, and the sun is happier in a monastery refectory than in a restaurant. Apples, bread, potatoes—from now on they will satisfy not just physical, but spiritual hunger. The Christian, and now every cultured person is a Christian, knows not only physical hunger and spiritual nourishment. For him the word is flesh and plain bread is a joy and a mystery.

*

Social distinctions and class conflicts pale before the present-day separation between friends and enemies of the word. It is truly the division between the sheep and the goats. I can almost physically feel the unclean goatish smell given off by the enemies of the word. This is the appropriate place for the final argument in every serious dispute: My adversary smells bad.

The separation of culture from the state is the most significant event in our revolution. The secularization of the state has not stopped at the separation of church and state, as the French Revolution understood it. The transformation of society has brought about a deeper secularization. The state now shows toward culture that singular attitude that is best conveyed by the term "tolerance." But at the same time we can observe a new type of relationship in which the state is connected with culture in much the same way as the Kievan princes were connected with the monasteries. The princes kept the monasteries to *give counsel*. That sums it up. The extraneous position of the state in relation to cultural values makes it totally dependent on culture. Cultural values adorn the state, giving it color, form, and perhaps even gender. Inscriptions on state buildings, tombs, and gates guarantee the state against the erosion of time.

Poetry is a plow, which turns over the earth so that the deep layers of time, the black earth, come to the surface. But there are periods when humanity, not satisfied with the present and nostalgic for the deep layers of time, longs like a plowman for the virgin soil of past ages. Revolution in art leads inevitably to classicism. Not because David gathered in Robespierre's harvest, but because this is what the earth is thirsting for.

You often hear people say: That's fine, but it belongs to yesterday. But I say: Yesterday has still to be born. It has not yet really existed. I want another Ovid, Pushkin, Catullus, I am not satisfied with the historic Ovid, Pushkin, Catullus.

It is indeed remarkable that everyone is involved with the poets and cannot get free of them. You might think: I've read it and that's enough. Far from it. The silver trumpet call of Catullus:

Ad claras Asiae volemus urbes

[Let us fly to the bright cities of Asia (Carmen 46)]

torments us and disturbs us more than any Futurist riddle. It doesn't yet exist in Russian. But it *has to* exist in Russian. I give an example from Latin verse because for the Russian reader this has long been felt as obligatory; the imperative sounds more clearly here. But the same is true of all sorts of poetry, so long as it is classical. It is felt to be something that has to be, rather than something that has already been.

So there has not yet been a single poet. We are free of the burden of memories. But in return, what a lot of forebodings: Pushkin, Ovid, Homer. When a lover fills the silence with a jumble of tender names and suddenly recalls that all this has already been, the words and the hair, the cock crowing outside the window already crowing in Ovid's *Tristia,* he is transfixed by the profound joy of recurrence, an intoxicating joy:

I drink the mutinous air like some dark water,
time is turned up by the plow, and the rose was earth.

[See "Heaviness, tenderness" on page 35.]

The poet does not fear recurrence then, and he is easily intoxicated by classical wine.

What is true for one poet is true for all. There is no need to set up any schools, no need to invent one's own poetics.

*

The analytic method when applied to words, movement, and form is an entirely legitimate and ingenious way of proceeding. In recent times destruction has become a purely formal precondition of art. Dissolution, decomposition, putrefaction—all this is still *la décadence.* But the decadents were Christian artists, in their way the last Christian martyrs. Baudelaire's "*Une Charogne*" is an outstanding example of Christian despair. But the deliberate destruction of form is quite another matter. Painless Suprematism. Rejection of the face of things. Calculated suicide out of curiosity. It is possible to take things apart and to put them together again: This may seem like a formal experiment, but in reality it is a dissolution of the spirit (incidentally, while mentioning Baudelaire, I should like to underline his importance as a devotee in the truest Christian meaning of the word *martyre.*)

*

A heroic era has dawned in the life of the word. The word is flesh and bread. It shares the fate of flesh and bread: suffering. People are hungry. The state is hungrier still. But there is something yet more hungry: time. Time wants to consume the state. We hear the trumpet call of the warning scribbled by Derzhavin on his slate. Whoever takes up the word and displays it to time as a priest displays the Eucharist, that man will be a second Joshua. There is nothing hungrier than the modern state, and a hungry state is more terrible than a hungry man. Compassion for the state that has denied the word—such is the social objective, the heroic task of the modern poet:

> Let's honor, too, the fateful burden
> the people's leader, all in tears, accepts.
> Honor the darkening load of power
> in its unbearable dead weight.
> Who has a heart, must hear your vessel,
> time, as it sinks to the seabed . . .
>> [See "Let's honor freedom's twilight, brothers"
>> on page 28.]

Do not demand from poetry any special corporeality, concreteness, materiality. That is the same revolutionary hunger, the impulse of a doubting Thomas. What need is there to touch with the fingers? And above all, why identify the word with the thing, the grass, the object that it signifies?

How can the thing be the master of the word? The word is Psyche. The living word does not signify the thing, but freely chooses as a dwelling place one thing or another, a signification, a corporeality, a beloved body. And the word wanders freely around the thing, as the soul wanders around the abandoned but unforgotten body.

What I have just said about corporeality sounds rather different if we are talking about imagery:

> *Prends l'éloquence et tords lui le cou!*

> [Take eloquence and wring its neck (Verlaine, "*Art poétique*")]

Write poetry without images if you can, if you know the art. The blind person recognizes a beloved face from the slightest touch of seeing fingers, and tears of joy, the true joy of recognition, spring from the eyes after a long absence. The poem lives through its inner image, the sonorous molding of form which precedes the writing of the poem. Not a single word is written but the poem already resounds, and what resounds is the inner image as it is heard by the poet:

> only the moment of recognition is sweet!
> [See "Tristia" on page 29.]

What we have now is kind of glossolalia. In a holy frenzy the poet speaks in the language of all ages, all cultures. Nothing is impossible. As the room of a dying person is open to all, so the door of the old world is wide open to the multitude. Suddenly everything has become common property. Come and take what you want. Everything is accessible: all the labyrinths, the secret places, the forbidden passages. The word has become not a seven-tubed but a thousand-tubed flute, through which the breath of all the ages blows at once. In glossolalia the most astonishing thing is that the speakers do not know the language they are speaking. They are speaking a completely unknown tongue. It seems to them and to others that they are speaking Greek or Chaldean. This is the very opposite of erudition. Contemporary poetry, however complex and intricate it may be, is naive:

> *Ecoutez la chanson grise . . .*
>
> [Listen to the grey song . . . (Verlaine, "*Ecoutez la chanson bien douce*")]

The synthetic poet of modernity seems to me to be not a Verhaeren but a Verlaine of culture. For him all the complexity of the old world is simply Pushkin's flute. Ideas, scientific systems, political theories sing in him just as nightingales and roses sang in his predecessors. They say that the cause of revolution is hunger in the interplanetary spaces. We need to scatter wheat through the ether.

Classical poetry is the poetry of revolution.

from FOURTH PROSE

In a certain year of my life, grown men of a tribe that I hate with all my mental powers and that I do not wish to belong to and never will, took it into their collective heads to perform a monstrous and disgusting ritual over me. This ritual bears the name of literary circumcision or dishonoring, and it is performed in accordance with the custom and calendar of the tribe of writers, the victim being designated by the tribal elders.

I must insist that the writer's trade as it has evolved in Europe and especially in Russia has nothing in common with the honorable title of Jew, of which I am proud. My blood, weighed down by the legacy of shepherds, patriarchs, and kings, rebels against the thieving zingaro ways of the tribe of writers. While I was still a child, I was kidnapped by a rowdy troop of unwashed Romani, who dragged me with them for years along their foul ways, vainly attempting to teach me their one and only art and trade: pilfering.

Writers are a race with a disgusting skin odor and the filthiest methods of cooking. They are a race who wander around and sleep on their own vomit, expelled from the towns, hounded through the villages, but always and everywhere close to the powers that be, who allot them a place in designated districts like prostitutes. For always and everywhere literature has the same function: It helps the leaders keep the soldiers obedient and it helps the judges mete out punishment to the victims of the law.

A writer is a cross between a parrot and a priest. He's a Polly in the highest sense of the word. If his owner is French, he speaks French, but if he's sold to a Persian he'll say "pretty Polly" or "sugar for Polly" in Persian. A parrot has no age; he doesn't know day from night. If he bores his owner, he gets a black cloth thrown over him, and that for literature is an ersatz night.

from JOURNEY TO ARMENIA

It was on the island of Sevan, remarkable for two outstanding architectural monuments of the seventh century, but also for the foxholes of a recently vanished race of lice-ridden anchorites, foxholes now thickly overgrown with nettles and thistles, and no more alarming than the neglected cellars of holiday homes, that I lived for a month, luxuriating in the situation of a lake four thousand feet above sea level and accustoming myself to the contemplation of two or three dozen tombs, scattered like flowers among the restored monastery dormitories.

Every morning on the dot of five, the lake teeming with trout boiled up as if a great pinch of soda had been thrown into it. This was a truly mesmeric seance of changing weather, as if some medium had let loose on the previously untroubled limestone water first a silly ripple, then a birdlike seething, and finally a crazy turbulence worthy of Lake Ladoga.

At this time I couldn't deny myself the pleasure of walking three hundred yards along the narrow beach path that lies opposite the dark shore of Giunei.

Here the Gokchai forms a strait five times as wide as the Neva. A glorious fresh wind whistled into the lungs. The clouds moved faster every minute, and in half an hour the waves made haste to print out by hand an incunabular Gutenberg Bible in bold script beneath a darkly frowning sky.

At least seventy percent of the island population were children. Like little animals they climbed all over the tombs of the monks, sometimes bombarding a peaceful log, seeing in its cold shuddering on the lake bed the convulsions of a sea serpent, sometimes collecting bourgeois toads from the damp thickets or else grass snakes with intricately patterned little feminine heads, sometimes chasing this way and that a panic-stricken ram that just couldn't understand who its poor body was incommoding and shook out the fat tail it had developed in a life of freedom.

The full-grown meadow grasses on the leeward hump of the island were so strong, so juicy, so self-confident that you wanted to run an iron comb through them.

The whole island is Homerically strewn with bones, relics of the local pilgrims' picnics. More than this, it is literally paved with the fiery red slabs of unnamed graves, some poking up, some shattered and some crumbling away.

At the very beginning of my stay, news reached us that builders on the long, gloomy spit of land at Tsamakaberd, digging down to lay the foundations of a lighthouse, had stumbled on an urn burial of the ancient Urartu people. I had already seen in the museum at Yerevan a skeleton hunched in a seated position inside a large clay amphora, with a little hole cut in the skull to let out the evil spirit.

Early in the morning I was woken by the clatter of a motorboat. The noise was marking time. Two mechanics were warming up the tiny heart of the convulsive engine and pouring oil on it. But no sooner was it fixed than its gabbling voice—something like "not Peter not Adam, not Peter not Adam"—faded and died away on the water.

Professor Khachaturian, his face sheathed with an aquiline skin, under which all the muscles and ligaments stood out neatly numbered and labeled with Latin names, was already walking up and down the jetty in a long black Ottoman-style coat. By profession both an archeologist and a pedagogue, he had spent most of his career as director of a secondary school, the Armenian *gymnasium* in Kars. On being invited to join the faculty at Yerevan, he had brought with him not only his allegiance to the Indo-European school of thought and a deep hostility to Marr's Japhetic fantasies, but also a remarkable ignorance of the Russian language and of Russia, where he had never been.

Managing somehow to converse in German, we got into the boat with comrade Karinian, the former chairman of the Armenian Central Executive Committee.

This self-satisfied, full-blooded man, condemned now to a life of inactivity, cigarette smoking and such dismal pastimes as the reading of Onguardist literature, was clearly finding it difficult to live without his official duties, and boredom had left its cloying kisses on his ruddy cheeks.

The engine muttered "not Peter not Adam" as if it was making a report to comrade Karinian; the island quickly dropped away behind us, stretching out its bearish spine with the octagons of its monasteries. The boat was escorted by swarms of midges, through which we sailed as through muslin over the milky morning lake.

We did indeed discover fragments of earthenware and human bones in the excavations, but also a knife handle with the mark of the old Russian firm of NN.

And it was with a feeling of reverence that I wrapped in my handkerchief a porous, limy, boxlike fragment from somebody's cranium.

Life on any island—Malta, Saint Helena, or Madeira—proceeds with a kind of dignified expectancy. This has its own charm, and its disadvantages. In any case, everyone is always occupied; they all tend to speak quietly and are more concerned for one another than on the mainland with its spacious roads and its negative freedom.

The aural cavity becomes more sensitive and acquires an additional helix.

It was my good fortune that on Sevan there was a whole gallery of wise old thoroughbreds—the venerable ethnographer Ivan Yakovlevich Sagatelian, the aforementioned archaeologist Khachaturian, and the life-loving chemist Gambarian.

I preferred their quiet company and coffee-impregnated conversations to the superficial talk of the young people, which as usual revolved around examinations and physical training.

Gambarian speaks Armenian with a Moscow accent. He has cheerfully and willingly Russified himself. His heart is youthful, his body lean and sinewy. Physically he is a most agreeable man and an excellent person to play games with.

He was anointed with some sort of military oil, as if he had just left the regimental chapel, but this doesn't prove anything and is often the case with the best Soviet people.

With women he is a chivalrous Mazeppa, caressing Maria with only his lips; with men he is the enemy of caustic wit and egoism, and if he gets into an argument, becomes as agitated as some Frankish fencer.

The mountain air rejuvenated him; he rolled up his sleeves and leapt for the volleyball net, manipulating the ball with his dry little hands.

What shall we say about the Sevan climate?

A golden coin of cognac in the secret cupboard of the mountain sun. The little glass column of the *dacha* thermometer was carefully passed from hand to hand. Doctor Herzberg was quite openly bored on this island of Armenian mothers. He seemed to me like the pale shadow of an Ibsenite problem, or else an actor from the Arts Theatre on holiday. The children showed him their narrow tongues, sticking them out for a split second, like fragments of bear meat.

And in due course hand, foot, and mouth disease appeared among us, transported in milk canisters from the distant shore of Zeinal where some kind of ex-Flagellants were living a silent life in gloomy Russian huts, having long ago stopped performing their religious rites.

As it turned out, the disease punished the sins of the fathers by confining itself to the godless boys of Sevan.

One after another the bristle-headed pugnacious children sank down in a high fever into the arms of women or onto pillows.

One day, in competition with the Young Communist Kh., Gambarian set out to swim all round the island of Sevan. His sixty-year-old heart wasn't up to it, and Kh., who was himself exhausted, was obliged to leave his comrade and return to the start, where he threw himself down half-dead on the pebbles. The scene was witnessed by the volcanic walls of the island fortress, which ruled out any possibility of mooring.

A panic ensued. There was no lifeboat on Sevan, though one had already been ordered.

People began rushing around the island, in all the pride of irreparable disaster. An unread newspaper dropped with a tinny clatter from someone's hands. The island began to feel sick, like a pregnant woman.

We had no telephone or pigeon post to communicate with the mainland. The boat had gone off to Yelenovka two hours previously and however hard we listened, we couldn't hear the faintest chuntering on the water.

When the rescue expedition led by comrade Karinian, armed with a blanket, a bottle of cognac and so on, brought back the numb but smiling Gambarian, whom they had picked up from a rock, he was greeted with applause. This was the most splendid hand clapping I have ever heard: They were applauding a man for not yet being a corpse.

On the fishermen's wharf at Noratus, where we were taken on an excursion blessedly free of choral singing, I was struck by seeing the carcass of a completely finished barge sticking up in its raw state on the shipyard rack. It was about the size of a good Trojan horse and in its fresh musical proportions it resembled a Ukrainian *bandura* case.

All around lay curly wood shavings. The earth was eaten away by salt, and little fish scales twinkled like specks of quartz.

Sitting in a row in the co-op restaurant, which was as Mein-Herz-Peter-the-Great logcabinish as everything else in Noratus, we were given copious helpings of a thick collective mutton-based cabbage soup. The workers noticed that we had no wine, so like true hosts they filled our glasses.

I drank a heartfelt toast to young Armenia with its orange houses, to its white-toothed people's commissars, to the sweat of horses and the stamping of queues, and to its mighty language in which we are not worthy to speak and so must skirt feebly around it:

water in Armenian: *dzhur*
village in Armenian: *gyur*

I shall never forget Arnoldi.

He got around on an orthopedic boot, but so pluckily that everyone envied him his way of walking.

The academic authorities of the island lived by the highway in Molokan Yelenovka, where in the penumbra of their central committee room the policeman's fishheads of gigantic pickled trout gazed bluely out.

And the visitors!

They were brought from Sevan with the speed of a telegram on an American yacht that cut through the water like a lancet—and Arnoldi stepped ashore, a storm of science, a Tamburlane of good nature.

I got the impression that there was a blacksmith living in Sevan who shod him, and that it was to chew the fat with him that Arnoldi used to disembark on the island.

There is nothing more enlightening and cheering than immersing yourself in a society of people of a quite different race, a race you respect and sympathize with, a race of which you can be vicariously proud. The fullness of life of the Armenians, their rough warmth, their noble readiness to work, their inexpressible revulsion in the face of any kind of metaphysics and their splendid familiarity with the world of real things—all this said to me: You are awake. Don't fear the time you live in. Don't be shifty.

Is this not because I was living among a people famed for their turbulent activity and yet living not by the clocks of railways or institutions, but by sundials such as the one I saw in the ruins of Zartnots Cathedral in the form of an astronomical wheel, or rose, carved into the rock?

IN AMONG THE NATURALISTS

Lamarck fought sword in hand for the honor of living nature. Do you think it was as easy for him to come to terms with evolution as for the scientific savages of the nineteenth century? In my opinion his swarthy cheeks were burning with shame for nature. He couldn't forgive it for that trifling business we call variability of species.

Forward! *Aux armes!* Let us wash off the dishonorable stain of evolution.

Reading the systematic naturalists (Linnaeus, Buffon, Pallas) has a splendid effect on our emotional equilibrium, rectifies our vision, and gives our soul a mineral, quartzlike calm.

Here is Russia as depicted by the great naturalist Pallas: Peasant women creating Mariona dye out of alum and birch leaves, lime-tree bark peeling off of its own accord to give bast for slippers and baskets, peasants using crude oil as medicine, Chuvash women jangling coins in their plaits.

Anyone who doesn't like Haydn, Glück, and Mozart won't understand the first thing about Pallas.

He transferred the rotundity and sweetness of German music to the plains of Russia. He picks Russian mushrooms with the white hands of the leader of an orchestra. Damp leather, decayed velvet—but split it open and you'll find the blue of the sky.

Anyone who doesn't like Haydn, Glück and Mozart won't understand a thing about Pallas!

Let's talk about the physiology of reading. A rich, inexhaustible, and apparently forbidden subject. Of all material objects, all physical bodies, the book is the object that inspires most trust in human beings. The book, set up on a lectern, is like a canvas stretched on a frame.

When we are fully absorbed in the business of reading, we marvel most at our native qualities, feeling a sort of delight at the classification of our different ages.

But if Linnaeus, Buffon, and Pallas enriched my mature years, I have a whale to thank for awakening in me a childish amazement at science.

It was in the Zoological Museum:

—drip, drip, drip

—not an atom of empirical experience.

Turn off the tap, will you!

That's enough!

I have signed a truce with Darwin and placed him on an imaginary bookshelf side by side with Dickens. If they had dinner together, there would be a third person there: Mr. Pickwick. You can't help being charmed by Darwin's jollity. He is an unintentional humorist. He is characterized (unfailingly) by a humor of situation.

But is jollity really a method for creative discovery or a proper instrument for experiencing life?

There is a Dantesque grandeur in Lamarck's reverse progress down the ladder of living beings. The lowest forms of organic existence are an inferno for humans.

The long grey antennae of a certain butterfly had a bearded structure and closely resembled the branches on the collar of a French academician or the silver palms laid on a tomb. The body was powerful, built like a little boat, the head insignificant, catlike.

Its eye-marked wings were of fine old admiral-quality silk, such as was seen at the battles of Chesme or Trafalgar.

And suddenly I caught myself wildly desiring to look at the world through the painted eyes of this monster.

Lamarck feels the great gaps between the classes. He hears the pauses and the syncopation in the evolutionary scale.

Lamarck wept his sight away into a magnifying glass. In natural history he is the only Shakespearian figure.

See how this flushed, half-respectable old gentleman rushes down the ladder of living beings, like a young man kindly treated at a meeting with the minister or made happy by his mistress.

No one, not even an inveterate mechanist, sees the growth of an organism as the result of a changing external environment. This would be far too crude. The environment simply invites the organism to develop. Its function can be seen as a certain favorable influence that is gradually and inevitably extinguished by the stern hand which seizes hold of the living body and rewards it with death.

So for the environment the organism is a probability, something desired or expected. And for the organism the environment is an inviting power. Not so much a container as a challenge.

When a conductor with his baton draws a theme from the orchestra, he is not the physical cause of the sound. This is already present in the score of the symphony, the spontaneous understanding of the performers, the crowded hall, and the disposition of the instruments.

There are fabulous animals in Lamarck. They adapt to the conditions of life. As in La Fontaine. The heron's legs, the duck's or swan's neck, the anteater's tongue, the asymmetrical or symmetrical construction of the eyes of certain fish.

You could say that La Fontaine prepared the way for Lamarck's teaching. His clever-clever moralizing, reasoning beasts provided splendid living material for a theory of evolution. They already shared out its directives between them.

The cloven-hooved reason of mammals clothes their feet in curved horn.

The kangaroo moves in logical leaps.

As Lamarck describes it, this marsupial consists of front legs that are weak, i.e. reconciled to their unnecessary status, back legs that are strongly developed, i.e. convinced of their importance, and a powerful thesis called a tail.

Children were already preparing to build sand castles by the plinth of the evolutionary theory of old man Krylov, i.e. Lamarck-La Fontaine. Finding a place of refuge in the Luxembourg Gardens, it became overgrown with balls and shuttlecocks.

What I like is when Lamarck chooses to be angry and the whole Swiss pedagogical tedium is smashed to pieces. The concept of "nature" is invaded by the Marseillaise!

Male ruminants clash foreheads. They have no horns yet. But the inner feeling aroused by anger directs "fluids" to the forehead and this assists in the formation of horn and bone.

I take off my hat to him. I make way for the teacher. May the youthful thunder of his eloquence never subside!

"Still" and "already" are the two shining lights in Lamarck's thought, the spermatozoa of evolutionary glory, the signalmen and pioneers of morphology.

He belonged to the race of old piano tuners, tinkling away with bony fingers in the mansions of others. All he was allowed was chromatic twists and childish arpeggios.

Napoleon allowed him to tune nature, because he saw it as imperial property.

In Linnaeus's zoological description one cannot fail to notice a causal link, indeed a sort of dependence on the fairground menagerie. The owner of a traveling circus, or a charlatan hired to give explanations, does his best to display his wares to best advantage. Enticing the public with their explanations, these people never thought of the role they would play in the formation of classical natural history. They lied unstoppably, spun out nonsense on an empty stomach, but at the same time they were carried away by their art. They were saved by luck, but also by their professional experience and the solid tradition of their craft.

As a boy in the little town of Uppsala, Linnaeus was bound to visit the fairs and listen to the explanations in the travelling menageries. Like all little boys, he was bowled over by the learned honcho with his boots and his whip, the doctor of fabulous zoology who sang the praises of the puma, waving his enormous red fists.

In likening the important works of a Swedish naturalist to the eloquence of a fairground loudmouth, I have not the slightest wish to belittle Linnaeus. I merely want to remind readers that a naturalist is by profession a storyteller, a public demonstrator of interesting new species.

The colored images of animals in Linnaeus's *System of Nature* could be hung next to pictures of the Seven Years' War or an oleograph of the Prodigal Son.

Linneaus painted his monkeys in the most touching colonial colors. He dipped his brush in Chinese lacquers and wrote with brown and red pepper, saffron, olive, and cherry juice. And he carried out his task nimbly and cheerfully, like a barber shaving a burgomaster or a Dutch housewife grinding coffee on her lap in a big-bellied coffee mill.

It's enchanting, the Columbuslike brightness of Linnaeus's monkey house.

It's Adam giving out certificates of excellence to the mammals with the help of a Baghdad conjurer and a Chinese monk.

The Persian miniature looks sideways out of timid, graceful, almond eyes.

Innocent and sensual, it is the best proof that life is a precious, inalienable gift.

I love Muslim enamels and cameos!

Continuing the comparison, I will say that the burning equine eye of the fair lady looks down aslant and graciously on the reader. The charred cabbage stumps of manuscripts crunch like the tobacco of Sukhumi.

How much blood was shed for these sensitive creatures! How the conquerors delighted in them!

The leopards have the cunning ears of schoolboys just punished.

The weeping willow has curled into a ball, it flows and floats.

Adam and Eve are conferring, dressed in the latest paradisal fashion.

The horizon is abolished. There is no perspective. A charming dimness. A fox grandly climbing the stairs and the feeling that the gardener is inclined toward the landscape and the architecture.

Yesterday I was reading Ferdowsi, and it seemed to me that a bumblebee was sitting on the book, sucking at it.

In Persian poetry winds blow like ambassadorial gifts from China.

It scoops up longevity with a silver ladle, bestowing it on whoever wants three or five thousand years. Thus it was that the emperors of the Jamshid dynasty were as long-lived as parrots.

The earth and the sky in the *Shahnameh* suffer from Basedow's disease—they are entrancingly goggle-eyed.

I got hold of Ferdowsi from the State Librarian of Armenia, Mamikon Artemyevich Gevorkian. I was brought a whole pile of little blue volumes—eight of them, I think. The words of the noble prose translation—in Mohl's French edition— were fragrant with attar of roses.

Mamikon chewed on his drooping governor's lip and chanted a few lines of Persian in his unpleasant camel voice.

Gevorkian is eloquent, intelligent, and polite, but his learning is excessively noisy and insistent and his speech heavy, like a lawyer's.

Readers are obliged to satisfy their curiosity on the spot, in the director's office, under his personal supervision, and the books served up on the desk of this satrap take on the taste of pink pheasant meat, bitter quail, musky venison, or cunning hare.

from CONVERSATION ABOUT DANTE

Così gridai colla faccia levata . . .
—*Inferno*, XVI, 76

Poetic speech is a hybrid process; it consists of two kinds of sonority, the first being the shift that we hear and feel in the instruments of poetic speech in its onward movement, and the second being the speech itself, that is to say the intonational and phonetic labor performed by these same instruments.

Conceived in this way, poetry is not a part of nature—not even the best, most precious part—and still less is it a reflection of nature—which would make a mockery of the law of identity—but it places itself with staggering independence in a new, extraspatial field of action, not so much narrating as acting out nature with the help of the instruments commonly known as images.

Poetic speech can only be described as sonorous in a very relative way, since what we hear in it is the combination of two lines, one of which is in itself absolutely mute, while the other, seen separately from its instrumental metamorphosis, is quite without significance or interest and can easily be paraphrased—which in my view is the surest sign of the absence of poetry, for where paraphrase is possible, the sheets remain unrumpled, so to speak, and poetry has not spent the night there.

Dante is a master of poetic instrumentation, not a fabricator of images. He is a strategist of transformation and combination, and least of all is he a poet in the "pan-European," culturally superficial meaning of that word.

Wrestlers locked together in the arena can serve as an emblem of instrumental transformation and resonance: "These naked, anointed champions, who strut around, showing off their impressive bodies, before coming to grips in the decisive struggle . . ."

Modern cinema, on the other hand, in its metamorphosis of the filmstrip tapeworm, turns out to be a cruel parody of the instrumentation of poetic speech, because the frames move forward without a struggle, simply succeeding one another.

Imagine something that has been understood, seized, and dragged out of the darkness in a language that is voluntarily and readily forgotten, as soon as the explanatory act of understanding and realization is complete . . .

In poetry only the realization of the understanding matters—this is in no way passive, nor does it reproduce or paraphrase. Semantic satisfaction is equivalent to the feeling of a command properly executed.

The waves/signals of meaning disappear, having fulfilled their function; the stronger and more supple they are, the less likely to linger.

Otherwise there is bound to be repetition, the hammering home of the readymade nails known as "cultural-poetic" imagery.

External, explanatory imagery is incompatible with the instrumental nature of poetry.

The quality of poetry is determined by the speed and decisiveness with which it embodies its executive intentions and commands in the uninstrumental, lexical, and often quantitative nature of verbal creation. One has to race across the full width of a river encumbered with mobile Chinese junks sailing in different directions—this is how the meaning of poetic speech is created. It is impossible to reconstitute this meaning, this itinerary, by asking the boatmen; they will not tell us how and why we leapt from one junk to the next.

Poetic speech is a carpet fabric that possesses a multitude of textile warps differing from one another simply in their performative coloration and in the musical score of the constantly changing commands of instrumental signaling.

It is the solidest of carpets, woven from water—a carpet in which the waters of the Ganges, taken as a textile theme, do not mingle with samples from the Nile or the Euphrates, but keep their distinctive color in their knots, their figures, their ornaments—but not in their design, since design is paraphrase yet again. Ornament is good in that it retains traces of its origins, like a *performed* piece of nature. It may be animal, vegetable, from the steppes, Scythia, or Egypt—anything at all, homegrown or barbaric—it is always capable of speaking, seeing, acting.

Ornament is of the stanza.

Pattern is of the line.

It is splendid, the hunger for verse of these old Italians, their animal, youthful appetite for harmony, their sensual lust for rhyme—*il disio!*

The mouth works, the smile sets verse in motion, the lips are red with wit and good cheer, the tongue presses trustingly against the palate.

The inward image of verse is inseparable from the countless succession of expressions that flicker across the face of the speaking tale teller in his emotion.

Indeed it is the art of speech that distorts our face, disturbs its peace, tears off its mask . . .

When I began studying Italian and had barely gotten to know its phonetics and its prosody, I suddenly realized that in the exertion of speaking the center of gravity had moved: It was closer to the lips, to the outside of the mouth. Suddenly the tip of the tongue was in the place of honor. Sound raced down to the floodgates of the teeth. And I was struck by something else—the infantile nature of Italian phonetics, its lovely childishness, its closeness to baby talk, a kind of original Dadaism:

> E consolando, usava l'idioma
> Che prima i padri e le madri trastulla:
> . . . .
> Favoleggiava con la sua famiglia
> De' Troiani, di Fiesole, e de Roma
> *(Paradiso,* XV, 122–26)

> [And soothing spake that speech / which first delighted fathers and mothers /
> . . . / would tell her household / about the Trojans, and Fiesole, and Rome" (in the prose translation of Philip H. Wicksteed)]

Do you want to be acquainted with the dictionary of Italian rhymes? Take a complete Italian dictionary and leaf through it at random . . . Everything rhymes. Every word is asking to be in a *concordanza.*

The abundance of matching words is marvelous. The Italian verb gathers strength as it progresses, it only lives in its ending. Every word hastens to explode, to fly off the lips, to depart, and make room for more.

When he needed to trace the circle of time for which a millennium is less than the twinkling of an eye, Dante introduced childish nonsense language into his astronomic, concert-hall, deeply public, preacher's vocabulary.

Dante's creation is above all the emergence in the world arena of the Italian speech of his time, as a whole, a system.

The most Dadaist of the Romance languages advances to the place of honor on the international stage.

NOTES

POEMS

9 *Batyushkov's conceit*: Konstantin Batyushkov (1787–1855): Poet, precursor of Russia's "golden age," author of the great elegy "Tasso Dying." He collapsed into insanity in 1821 and wrote no further poetry. See "Batyushkov" on page 66.

12 *poor Eugene*: The hero-victim of Alexander Pushkin's narrative poem "The Bronze Horseman: A Petersburg Story," published in 1837.

13 *The Admiralty*: This building served as a central point in the planning of St. Petersburg.

15 *Rachel once stood*: Elisabeth Félix (1821–1858), or Mademoiselle Rachel: nineteenth-century French actress, famous for her performance in the title role of Racine's *Phèdre*.

19 *How these vain veils . . .*: A line from Racine's *Phèdre*.

20 *How the splendor of these veils*: The poem references both Racine's *Phèdre*, which is quoted in the longer lines, and Euripides' *Hippolytus*.

24 *In a deep sleigh, with straw spread for a litter*: The poem is addressed to the poet Marina Tsvetaeva (1892–1941).
Uglich: The scene of the murder of the young prince Dmitry Ivanovich, Ivan the Terrible's son, in 1591. See Pushkin's *Boris Godunov*.

25 *Doubting the wonder of the resurrection*: The poem is addressed to Marina Tsvetaeva, whom Mandelstam met at Koktebel in the Crimea and again in the northern town of Vladimir, where this poem is set.

27 *Tauris*: Ancient name for Crimea.

29 *Tristia*: Latin meaning "sorrows" and the title of a collection of verse epistles by Ovid (43 BC–18 AD), written while he was in exile from Rome in Tomis.

48 *Slate Pencil Ode*: This poem echoes the eight-line stanza about the destructive river of Time that the great eighteenth-century poet Gavrila Derzhavin (1759–1762) scribbled onto a slate when he was close to death. A later version omits the second half of stanza six and the first half of stanza seven, using as an epigraph the lines "For

us, only the voice explains / all that was scratching, struggling there." See note below for page 125.

50   *in the flint road of the old song*: A reference to Lermontov's poem "I Go Out on the Road Alone."

60   *I drink to the asters of wartime*: In this poem of mocking defiance, Mandelstam highlights some of the high-society features of his early poems which were condemned by Soviet critics.

62   *Dziękuję, pani*: "Thank you, sir" (Polish).

66   *Batyushkov*: See note for "No, not the moon" on page 9.

68   *We too were there*: A traditional ending for folk tales.

69   *Cold spring. Fearful Crimea with no grain*: In 1933 Mandelstam revisited the Crimea, now ravaged like the nearby Kuban and Ukraine by the famine of forced collectivization.

      Wrangel: Pyotr Nikolayevich Wrangel, White Army general in the Civil War of 1917–22.

71   *The apartment—quiet as paper*: In 1933 the Mandelstams were finally allocated a small apartment in Moscow. This poem appears to be connected to the indignation Mandelstam felt when Pasternak congratulated him on having a place where he could write.

73   *We live without touching the homeland beneath us*: This poem, recited to a number of people in private, was mainly responsible for Mandelstam's arrest in 1934.

      Ossetian: Stalin's ancestors were possibly from Ossetia in the Caucasus.

77   *After long-fingered Paganini*: Written after a concert by the violinist Galina Barinova.

      chenchurá: This word remains obscure.

      Marina Mniszek: A Polish noblewoman who briefly became the empress of Russia in 1606. Mandelstam associated her with Marina Tsvetaeva.

78   *We are still full of life up to the brim*: Originally titled "Children's Haircut."

80   *Kama*: Mandelstam and his wife traveled on the Kama River to and from Cherdyn.

82   *Stanzas*: These stanzas reflect on Mandelstam's relation to Soviet power. Stanza three alludes to his attempted suicide in Cherdyn.

87   *My goldfinch*: Note that the Russian word for "goldfinch" is almost identical to the word for "dandy."

93   *Yeast*: i.e., poetry.

94   *You've not died yet, and still you're not alone*: In another version of this poem "you" is   replaced with "I" in the first two stanzas.

PROSE

113   *The Noise of the Times:* These sketches of the world of Mandelstam's childhood and youth were first published in 1925. The title could be read as referring to these specific times or to time in general.

118   *The Bookcase*: The final section of this chapter, mainly concerned with the poet Nadson, has been omitted.

122   *The Word and Culture*: Published in a Soviet journal in 1921, then with cuts in a collection of Mandelstam's writings about poetry in 1928. The translation here is based on the original version.
      Little he ever understood . . .: Lines referring to Ovid from Pushkin's long poem "The Gypsies," translated by Antony Wood.

125   *scribbled by Derzhavin on his slate*: Just before dying, the poet Gavrila Derzhavin wrote a brief poem on a slate:

>   Time's river in its rushing course
>   carries away all human things,
>   drowns in oblivion's abyss
>   peoples and kingdoms and their kings.
>   And if the trumpet and the lyre
>   should rescue something, small or great,
>   eternity will gulp it down
>   and it will share the common fate.

      See the "Slate Pencil Ode" on page 48.

128   *Fourth Prose*: "Fourth Prose," a violent satire against the Soviet literary establishment, was provoked by an incident of 1929, when Mandelstam had been wrongly accused of plagiarism in a translation of *Till Eulenspiegel*. According to Nadezhda Mandelstam, the resulting polemic had "really opened M.'s eyes to what was happening around

us," thus helping him to start writing poetry again after a long silence. "Fourth Prose" was never published in the Soviet Union.

129   *Journey to Armenia*: Mostly written in 1931 and first published in 1933, *Journey to Armenia* records the Mandelstams' visit to Armenia in the summer of 1930, made with the help of Nikolay Bukharin. Of the two sections translated here, "In Among the Naturalists" is largely devoted to Mandelstam's very personal reading in Armenia of some classics of biological writing.

Sevan: Sevan is now a peninsula in a lake of the same name (previously called Gokchai).

130   *Marr's Japhetic fantasies*: The Georgian linguist Nikolai Marr (1865–1934), whose theories of the origins of language were highly influential in the Soviet Union under Stalin. His Japhetic theory related languages of the Caucasus to the Semitic languages of the Middle East.

133   *bandura*: A plucked stringed instrument somewhat like a cross between a lute and zither.

134   *Pallas*: Peter Simon Pallas (1741–1811), a Prussian naturalist who worked extensively in Russia.

140   *Conversation about Dante*: This essay was written at the beginning of the 1930s, mainly at Koktebel in the Crimea. The definitive typescript, dated 1933, was first published in Moscow in 1967.

Cosi gridai colla faccia levata: "Thus I cried with face uplifted" (in the prose translation of John Aitken Carlyle). The context is an attack on the "pride and excess" of Florence.

instruments: The word *orudie* and its derivatives, translated here as "instruments," "instrumentation" etc., refers to the active processes or devices (e.g. prosody) that Mandelstam sees as propelling poetic creativity.

These naked, anointed champions . . . : A free translation of *Inferno* XVI, 22–24.

OSIP EMILIEVICH MANDELSTAM (1891–1938) grew up in a Jewish family in St. Petersburg, with long visits to Western Europe as a student. Associated, like Anna Akhmatova, with the Acmeist group of poets, he remained in Russia after the Revolution, but was increasingly at odds with the Soviet regime. In 1919 he met his wife-to-be, Nadezhda Yakovlevna Khazina, who was responsible for preserving much of his later poetry. The couple led a precarious and nomadic life; Mandelstam found it increasingly difficult to publish. He was exiled to Voronezh for three years, then in 1938 he was arrested a second time, sentenced to hard labor, and died in eastern Siberia, leaving behind some of the most glorious poems and essays ever written.

PETER FRANCE has published widely on French, Russian, and comparative literature, including the *Oxford Guide to Literature in English Translation*. His translations of the Chuvash poet Gennady Aygi—*Time of Gratitude*, *Field-Russia*, and *Child-and-Rose*—are available from New Directions.